Cor.

Preface 5

India's Golden Ages: 1000 AD
and 2020 AD 13

Industrial Jobs in Rural India 37

Can India see itself as the Next
China? 59

Micro credit 85

Education in Rural India 117

Vocational Training 139

Renewable Energy 157

Creation of new towns 181

Second Green Revolution 203

Focus on the Poorest of the Poor 225

India Calling 255

Conclusion 289

India At The Crossroads

This book attempts to explore practical ways for India to overcome its difficulties. These suggestions are within India's economic means. The book covers the following chapters and topics: public sector and private sector industries, can India see itself as the next China?, microcredit, education in rural India, vocational training, climate change and alternative sources of energy, creation of new towns with infrastructure laid out to seamlessly grow to mini-new cities, second Green Revolution, centrally administered districts, foreign direct investment (FDI), action needed in the 12th Five-Year plan, dream can be turned to reality. The determination of leaders and people are required. How India will change in the 21st century in the globalized world will be examined.

India At The Crossroads

Preface

India At The Crossroads

Preface

India has improved its foreign exchange position considerably. But weak areas remain with jobs, infrastructure, industries and farming in the rural areas of India, where majority of India's people live.

This book is about India's need for infrastructure development. India needs new bridges, airports, railway stations, sea ports, New Towns with pre-laid growth oriented infrastructure. Although India's growth rate is nearly 5.5%, it needs innovative ways of foreign investment in infrastructure and industries.

The most essential need in India is to generate jobs, especially in rural regions, and to move forward at a faster pace. India has lost many opportunities, but if the current opportunity is lost, India will never be able to catch up.

With WTO compulsion (facilities), Chinese companies not only sell to the West but they are increasingly exporting cheap manufactured goods to India. Multinational companies also export manufactured goods to India from China - instead of manufacturing in India.

Compared to India, China is more integrated with the world economy. India's share of world trade is well below its potential. China's participation in world trade is six times as large.

Poor people in villages have hardly enjoyed India's

phenomenal growth. The conditions of the day-to-day life faced by the majority of rural populace are pathetic with harsh reality of poverty, neglect and helplessness. Along with industrial growth, India should simultaneously alleviate rural poverty by diverse initiatives.

Many people blame democracy for slow progress in India as compared to China. It is true to some extent. But, whatever and whenever the government of India wants to do something, it gets it done. There are many reasons for this slow progress including corruption and laid back attitude. Delays in implementing many projects have wasted a lot of money.

Until very recently, annual foreign direct investment in China by overseas companies was five times larger than their investment in India. But India is slowly catching up.

Rural Indians should have the similar option of living and working in urban India on jobs in non-agricultural sector. If we do not want the realities of today's India to persist into the future, a generation and two hence, then we should have majority of rural Indians engaged in labour-intensive industries in New Towns in the hubs of village clusters.

India needs to make sure that there is time bound progress in rural areas. If we do not improve the economic condition of rural people, slums will keep increasing in big cities. The government's aim ought

Preface

to be to see that there are no slums left in semi-urban kasbahs and urban areas by 2020.

India's rural income is very low. If the poverty is attacked on all these fronts as discussed, in the next ten years people will be making $5 a day in rural India. This will be real progress. Many people will have jobs in New Towns and the income of rural India will increase manifold. This book is a blue print for improving India's economy at an accelerated pace.

There is a need for industrial jobs in rural India. India needs expansion of public sector enterprises in addition to private sector industries to provide jobs - especially in rural locations. The Indian industrial sector is very small compared to the Chinese industrial spread.

India's public sector is very healthy now. With foreign collaboration, public sector companies should multiply their manufactured goods.

Microcredit for the poor can create self-employment and generate income. For generations, people in India have engaged in small businesses for self-employment. In rural India most people take recourse to self-employment in different fields.

By providing some capital through banks, governments can help poor people advance their small businesses with small loans. This should be done on a large scale as soon as possible.

India now has a new Right to Education Act. The poor

infrastructure of schools in rural areas has resulted in fairly high dropout rates. Many schools in rural India lack female teachers and do not have washroom facilities for female teachers and students. Fifty percent of students leave school before the primary fifth grade.

Many times school teachers do not even show up at work. Rural India needs more teachers or teachers' assistants. The number of teachers should be increased considerably for students to receive an acceptable quality of education. The teacher helper could be paid by the National Rural Employment Guarantee Act (NREGA).

India does not spend sufficient money on training its technical students to make India a manufacturing hub. Sustained vocational education and training hardly exists in India, while China's network of technical training facilities is extensive.

A well structured vocational education system will increase job prospects. General vocational training classes should be started in schools as a part of the curriculum -- because a large number of students will drop out at the primary level. Once a week, classes should be devoted to vocational training — encouraging students to learn to use their hands and working with tools.

In the Russian Federation and still in former Soviet Republics of Eastern Europe and Central Asia, every man has a personal tool kit for basic carpentry, plumbing and electrical trouble shooting needs. They

Preface

do not call in technicians to their homes and work places unless, a situation on hand is clearly beyond their early training and subsequent experience.

Indian vocational training initiatives for drop out students should aim at ensuring their continuing attendance with short duration courses of three to six months, to get them started on technical trades. Let us build this system from the ground up on a very extensive scale.

In rural India approximately 350 million people do not have electricity. Large-scale use of clean energy technology would not only reduce pollution, but would create millions of production jobs.

Currently, solar and wind energy equipment are in short supply throughout the world. Our public sector units have the base of manufacturing. Electricity can transform remote villages, helping them leapfrog from the Dark Ages to the twenty-first century. Children can study at night after they have completed their chores. With solar and wind energy, payback in terms of direct benefits begin from the very first year they are put into effect.

There is a need for creation of New Towns with inbuilt potential to grow. India has about 70% (900 million people) spread over 600,000 villages. The country needs at least 600 new urban growth centres to provide employment opportunities to 100 million of people who now live in villages. Most of these New Towns should be situated about an hour bus drive (or one to two hour bicycle ride) from the villages.

India At The Crossroads

India should build hundreds of New Towns and base the economy of the new urban centres on a combination of manufacturing, service providing and agriculture.

India needs to develop holistic plans of action for water shortage and rainfall instability. Increasing water efficiency in agriculture is needed with new irrigation strategies and increased attention to droughts through improved secure water storage. Increasing the productivity of agriculture without wasting water, getting more crop per drops is imperative.

The central government must directly assist the poorest districts of poor states. The most backward districts should be run by an administrator appointed and funded by the central government, directly under the control of the Prime Minister.

The administrator would be responsible for the delivery of selected public goods until they are self-sufficient and prosperous. This would provide people with jobs, owning small businesses, provision of water, road and at least basic sanitation.

India has improved its foreign exchange position considerably. This country's foreign investment policy has been formulated with a view to inviting and encouraging investment flow into India. The Government of India welcomes the investment (FDI) from other countries.

India's Golden Ages: 1000 AD and 2020 AD

India At The Crossroads

India's Golden Ages: 1000 AD and 2020 AD

India has a long and proud history. The world community recognises that India has already arrived onto the world stage. In the words of US President Obama, speaking of his recent visit to India: "India is not a rising power anymore, India has emerged". India's recent economic performance is once again attracting world's attention. Democracy, economy, industrialization and social changes are transforming India.

The 'Golden' Past

India was home to one of the earliest human civilizations. The country had a well irrigated system and a sophisticated artisan manufacturing sector. The earliest reservoir and dam for irrigation was built in Saurashtra. The art of navigation was born on the river Sindh (Indus) 5000 years ago. The very word "Navigation" was derived from the Sanskrit term NAVGATIH. It is clear that India's economy was considered very advanced at that time. The Indus Valley Civilization flourished between 3300 and 2000 BC in India. The ruins of its cities are extraordinary and suggest a very sophisticated economy that was able to support major urban areas. The Indus Valley civilization was more remarkable for their attention to urban planning. Their towns appeared to be built around standardized plans. Most modern Indian towns (mini-new cities) in the hubs of village clusters would do well to follow their example. The average Indian of the Golden Era would have enjoyed a standard of living that was far higher than that of their contemporaries in other parts of the world.

There were many great people who recognized the prosperity and achievements and said great things about India.

Albert Einstein (1879 -1955) said about India:

> We owe a lot to the Indians, who taught us how to count, without which no worthwhile scientific discovery could have been made.

Mark Twain (1835-1910) said about India:

> India is the cradle of the human race, the birth place of human speech, the mother of history, the grandmother of legend and the great grandmother of tradition.

Brilliant mathematicians, astronomers and economists

India's top position was not limited to trade, efficiently run administration, or economics alone. Indian mathematicians, astronomers, metallurgists and physicians were arguably among the best in the world and were held in high regard. Ancient India had produced a line of brilliant philosopher and mathematicians. Aryabhatta was the greatest mathematician and scholar in astronomy in ancient India (Gupta dynasty). During the Gupta dynastic era in ancient India (around 350 AD), there was unprecedented improvement in the fields of science, mathematics and astronomy.

India invented the numeric system. Indian mathematicians made extraordinary innovations, including the concept of zero, the basis of the numerical system that we use today. Astronomer and mathematician Aryabhatta also made remarkably accurate estimates of the circumference of the earth and of the ratio Pi. All this, a thousand years before Copernicus and Galileo. He calculated the value Pi to 3.1416 close to the actual value Pi (3.14159). But his greatest contribution was his innovation of the concept of zero. His other works include algebra, arithmetic, trigonometry, quadratic equations and the sine table.

Aryabhata (476–550 AD) was the first in the line of great mathematician-astronomers from the classical age of Indian mathematics and Indian astronomy. He talked about the position of the planets in relation to its movement around the sun. He was able to work out that the earth is spherical and that it rotates on its axis. He even computed the circumference of the earth as 24835 miles -- which is close to modern day calculation of 24900 miles. This remarkable man was a genius and continues to baffle many mathematicians today.

Bhaskaracharya was another great mathematician and astronomer. He calculated the time taken by the earth to orbit the sun as 365.258756484 days in the

12th century. Bhaskaracharya supplied the correct answer for division by zero as well as rules for operating with irrational numbers. (If zero is divided by any number or multiplied by any number, the result is zero. If any number is divided by zero, the result is infinity.)

Ayurveda is the earliest school of medicine known to humans. Charaka, the father of Indian medicine consolidated Ayurveda 2500 years ago. Today Ayurveda is fast regaining its rightful place in our civilization. Sushruta, the father of surgery, conducted complicated procedures dealing in India with cataracts, artificial limbs, fractures, urinary stones, plastic surgery, caesarean section and brain surgery 2,600 years ago. Over 125 surgical instruments were in use. The use of anaesthesia was also known in ancient India. The World's first university was established in Takshashila north-west of Rawalpindi in 700BC. More than 10,500 students from all over the world studied more than 60 subjects there.

Ancient Universities of India

The Gupta rulers encouraged higher learning by patronizing centers of higher education at Nalanda, Takshashila, Ujjain, Vikramshila and Vallabhi. Each University specialized in a particular field of study. During the Gupta period, India became a centre for higher studies attracting scholars from all parts of India and from several foreign countries.

Vikramshila University imparted education in many subjects. Vallabi University was situated in modern Gujarat. The university specialized in many branches of learning such as Arthashastra, Law and Medicine.

Nalanda University offered a choice of many subjects for study. Panini, the famous Sanskrit grammarian, Kautilya who wrote Arthashastra, Charaka the famous physician of ancient India, and Chandragupta Maurya were the products of this university. The Taxila town was already famous in about 300 B.C., at the time when Alexander the Great had come to India.

India had an extraordinary economic, intellectual and cultural influence throughout the ancient world.

The Indian Renaissance by Sanjeev Sanyal

> In a (many) ways, India's place in the ancient world was similar to that which is occupied by the United States today. India was not only the dominant centre of economics and cultural activity, but also a magnet for various groups of people who came to seek either fortune or refuge from persecution. Not many people realize that India is host to one of the oldest Jewish communities in the world. (page 11)

India is the world's largest democracy now. Although modern images of India often show poverty and lack of development, India was the richest country on earth until the time of British invasion in the early 17th century, Christopher Columbus was attracted to India's wealth.

India has gone into decline because of its lack of cultural openness, spirit of entrepreneurship to new ideas and technologies. India did not keep up with the times. When India gained independence in 1947, its share in the world GDP had declined to barely 4%.

Liberalized economic policy in 1991

In 1991 India decided to liberalize its economy and since then it has improved its economy considerably. After independence from 1947 to 1990 the country was held down by self-imposed constraints that gave India underdeveloped and low international stature. Liberalization has clearly improved India's economic potential. The shift in 1991 was changing economic policies and all aspects of life from old inward-looking economic regime to opening out to the world. This also coincided with the collapse of communist Soviet Union in the early 90's. Indian economics and politics were influenced by communist Soviet Union prior to 1991. After 1991, India gradually improved its relations and trade with USA. The fact that it coincided with the communications revolution: cable television, mobile telephones, and the internet (in which India holds an advantage), a large number of Indians began to believe in their country again.

India is now at the crossroads. The country boasts highly competitive private companies, a booming stock market, and a modern well-disciplined financial sector. India has lowered trade barriers and tax rates, broken state monopolies, encouraged competition, and opened up to the rest of the world. India is poised at a key moment in its history. Rapid growth is likely to continue – and even accelerate. But India cannot take its progress for granted. Public debt is high, which discourages investment in needed infrastructure.

As India appears to be finally emerging as a global power, rich and middle class people are full of enthusiasm and aspirations. Unfortunately, this euphoria often tends to make these social classes even less concerned about the plight of the poor and the deprived. It is a perplexing mystery how people can ignore this painfully obvious reality when discussing India's tremendous economic success.

India needs labour intensive industries

India has not adapted the typical Asian and Chinese strategy -- exporting labour-intensive, low-price manufactured goods to North America and Europe and is far behind China – India has relied on its domestic market more than exports, consumption more than investment, services more than industry, and high-tech more than low-skilled manufacturing. This strategy hasn't helped much in creating jobs, especially in rural areas. The most oppressive fact about the conditions in rural India is the scarcity of employment opportunity. Economic development affects only a tiny part of India's population, with a Western standard of consumption, leaving the rest at the subsistence level.

Unlike China which has manufactured and exported luxury items first, India's rich and middle class have consumed a lot of these luxury items themselves. In addition to cars and expensive houses, they can afford drivers to escort them and servants to do their domestic work. Some people believe that within a span of a few generations prosperity will filter down to the lowest socio economic levels. A very large number of people are not particularly warm to this idea for a few reasons. The rich and middle class in India depend on cheap labour in order to enjoy a luxurious lifestyle.

Small traders; restaurant owners; shopkeepers (sellers of fruits, vegetables, meats and fish), depend on cheap labour. Most of these small shopkeepers and traders are making a lot of money because they are situated at strategic places (in the markets of urban areas). They depend on cheap labour and the majority of them do not pay income tax, which would improve the lives of those less fortunate. Also, nearly 10% of India's work force is employed by the organized sector, where through collective bargaining they have managed to raise their wages much above what they could earn elsewhere. Thus, India's organized labour is very expensive as compared to that of China, meanwhile a large percentage of India's population is unemployed and starving.

Organized sector has job security and higher wages

Workers employed by the private sector, service industry and manufacturing by the public sector, Central government, States and municipal government employees manage to get higher wages. At many places of employment, workers receive wages three to four times higher and have job security. Even corrupt employees are protected by the system. It is indisputable that second and third generation labourers in the organized sector are much better off than their predecessors and their children are well educated and in better jobs. The industrial sector in India is highly unionized, and these unions are preventing the absorption of labour by keeping industrial wages at an artificially high level.

In the book *'Why Poverty Persists in India'*, authors Mukesh Eswaran and Ashok Kotwal write:

> In India, as in the rest of the world, the poor are those who have nothing else to sell but their labour. But even among workers there are differences. Less than ten percent of India's labour force works for the organized sector where, through collective bargaining, they have managed to raise their wages much above what they could earn elsewhere. The white and blue collar workers employed in large manufacturing and service establishments such as Siemens (multinationals), Tatas (domest ic private corporations), railways and banks (service industries in the public sector), Bharat Heavy Electrical (public enterprises) fall into this category. It is possible for workers to get high wages because their employers do not operate in competitive market and so are able

to pass on the higher wage cost to the consumers by charging higher prices. These workers are hardly poor. By the poor we mean the workers competing in the labour market of agriculture and in the informal service sectors (e.g. hawkers, street vendors) throughout India. (page 120)

Majority of rural Indians unemployed or underemployed

Millions of people search for jobs outside the villages in cities, accepting any wage that is offered to them. India's rural economy is stagnant. Rural India has cheap labour ready to hire for any reason. In India, tens of millions live in slums and come from rural areas in search of jobs. There are over 72,000 slums in India and roughly half of urban India lives in slums in big cities like Mumbai and Delhi. What India needs is a proactive all-round development strategy and not one that happens by default. Yet the majority of Indian intellectuals and practically every political leader make no time to address these concerns.

Poor people in villages have hardly enjoyed India's phenomenal growth. The truth is that this growth-rate in India is accompanied by poverty. In terms of the economy, India is still very low on the International scale. The growth has not translated in terms of employment. Reasons for the scarcity of jobs are lack of industries, bank loans, infrastructure, education, vocational training and indifference of the democratic institutions for a poor man.

The Socialist pattern of society was the most harmful policy which the government followed from 1950 to 1990: restricting industrial licensing, quotas for raw material and imported items, high tariffs and other trade barriers, high tax rates, and almost closing India to foreign investment. The most damaging industrial policy was reserving around 800 industries, designated "small-scale industries" (SSI), for tiny companies that were unable to compete against the large firms of competitor nations of the world. Large private and public firms were barred from making products such as garments, toys and shoes, all the products that helped East Asia create millions of jobs. China's industries and export of garments and toys, grew into big, industries. India has now opened up these sectors to large firms in the last 10 years, after a lot of harm done to the industrial sector and export of these products.

India has remained an overwhelmingly poor country. In India the problem lies in tapping into the enormous productive potential of the people. Providing loans to millions of people whose rural livelihood is based on agriculture, craftsmanship, cottage or small-scale industries with microloans remains a challenge. India should start by extending the employment guarantee scheme in rural India, not only in the agriculture field but also in other fields such as: education (teacher and librarian assistants), and healthcare (doctor and nurse intern and paramedical assistants). These assistants can be employed at a minimum, uniform wage for 300 days a year, available on demand. India should give this top priority.

Reforms of 1991 finally allowed India's integration into the global economy, and laid the groundwork for its high growth today. The chief architects of this reform were the Prime Minister Narasimha Rao and the finance minister, Manmohan Singh, who is now the Prime Minister. The economy grew immediately; growth rose, inflation plummeted, and exports and currency reserves shot up.

India has improved its competitiveness considerably: there has been a telecommunications revolution, interest rates have come down and capital is plentiful. Although, conservative managers of the nationalized banks still refuse to lend to small manufacturers, especially to rural people as microloans without any collateral. Growth is being driven by services and domestic consumption. Consumption accounts for 64% of India's GDP compared to 42% for China.

China's state driven economy

There is a total and severe contrast between India's entrepreneur driven growth and China's state model. China's success is largely based on exports by state enterprises or foreign companies. India's development so far has not created the required number of jobs. India's high growth has not been accompanied by a labour-intensive industrial revolution that could transform the lives of the tens of millions of Indians still trapped in rural poverty.

In China tens of millions of jobs are created in towns in the hubs of village clusters. China creates an endless flow of low-end (and now high-end) manufacturing jobs by exporting goods such as toys and clothes and other textile items. Their better educated fellow citizens export knowledge services and manufactured goods to rest of the world. India's industry share is very weak and is only 27% of India's GDP as compared to 46% in China. Indian industry is absent, especially in the rural areas where the majority of its people live. In terms of actual US dollars, China's manufacturing industry is five times more than India's and China's export is many times more.

When you compare Asia's two rising BRICS (Brazil, Russia, India, China, South Africa) giants, China and India, China comes out on top in virtually every measure. Meanwhile India has yet to come up into the ranks of the world's top 10 economies. China's per capita income is about four times that of India: $1,400 compared to $6,100 in China.

With China's cheap manufacturing cost and WTO facility, they have taken over the American and European market. Now they are in a process of taking over Indian market.

Chinese public sector industries in collaboration with multinational industries are manufacturing goods at very cheap prices. The public sector industries themselves are producing manufactured goods in completion with multinational industries at much cheaper prices.

China used it's "fait accompli" authority to do things at an accelerated speed and assure foreign private enterprise an open door policy. China's government extends a welcome mat to foreign investors -- on its own terms. Multinational have greater choices in China. Provinces and China's central government encourage their investment. China relied on Chinese emigrants to provide capital. The welcoming of the overseas Chinese paid many dividends. These policies have brought China lots of jobs and made China a prosperous country. To a great extent, China has solved the problem of feeding the hungry millions. In contrast, India has shunned its diaspora until recently, surely one of the most self-defeating policies adopted by the Indian state. Although, in the past decade, overseas Indians have begun to have a voice in India

Industrial Revolution as it was experienced by the West was usually led by one industry. It was textile exports in the United Kingdom, and railways in the United States. At present India too have many industry engines that could fuel its takeoff and transform its economy. In addition to software and business-process outsourcing exports, there are other sectors also. Export of garments, toys, shoes, other leather products and more labour-intensive industry by large, medium and small private sector and public sector industries. India is already exporting cars, car parts, pharmaceutical goods, heavy engineering, and other materials (industrial goods). Hundreds of additional items can be added for export. This could provide jobs to millions of rural people.

Lokpal Bill will be introduced in the current session of parliament. At present, accountability in India is almost impossible and corruption is rampant. The most unfortunate aspect of corruption in India is that it is widely accepted as an unavoidable feature of Indian life. Under British rule, corruption was very little and corrupt people were scared to take bribes. Now there is a much greater tolerance for corruption, as an essential part of India's democracy.

Corruption causes fiscal drain, lower investment and reduces productivity. Reduction in corruption can significantly increase the investment ratio and enhance growth several times. The national output, employment and rate of return on projects will improve considerably. India is in a poverty trap because of corruption. Projects of infrastructure cost several times more. Adverse economic effects of corruption can be felt on small enterprises and overall growth of employment in the economy. In small industries, where most employment is created, corruption raises costs and reduces profits because the owner of the industry has to make payments that do not contribute to productivity or output but are essential for their survival.

There are many sensible steps that can be taken to improve governance, the areas where government touches most people's lives. Cities have done better than villages. Some states have done better than others. Indian economy has not created jobs commensurate with its rate of growth. Only a small fraction of Indians are employed in the modern, unionized sector. Hundreds of millions are unemployed or underemployed. One of the primary reasons for these failures is labour laws which need to be reformed, corruption must be eliminated and population should be controlled immediately. Like China, a one child policy should be put in place.

Millions of cross border illegal immigrants coming from neighbouring countries to India should be sent back and stopped. In USA, Canada and Europe when they find even one illegal immigrant, they make a lot of noise, especially the press and the government checking the loop hole. In India where Quarter of a billion people are unemployed or underemployed, these illegal people take away the lively hood from the Indian people. There are lobbies influencing the government for these illegal immigrants. These lobbies should not be allowed to influence the government decisions.

India will reach its greatness only when every Indian has access to a job, a good school, a working health clinic, and clean drinking water. Fortunately, half of India's population is under the age of 25 years. This will translate into abundance of labour and a boom for industry, if these youngsters receive vocational training. This time it also means that the labour market is teeming with the unemployed. In the last twenty years the workforce has increased by nearly 65% but organized employment remains stagnant.

Yet India cannot take its golden age for granted. If it does not continue down the path of reform and bring governance up to par with other successful countries, then a critical opportunity will be lost.

In spite of the fact, that the majority of people in India are extremely poor, it is still a golden age for 20% of Indians. Some people are enjoying wealth and power, which Indians have not experienced for centuries. A very large number of people are making money by fair or false means. Successive governments have continued with myopic thinking. Unless we do something drastic for the majority of rural poor, things are going to be grim for India. India lost its will to push ahead with those enlightened policies that Gandhi, Nehru and their contemporaries had in mind. Rather than spending a lot of money on infrastructure and creating jobs in rural India, India's governments over the years have spent money on luxuries (according to Indian standard and economic conditions). India should realize that the biggest driving force of the market is the purchasing power of ordinary people, derived from employment growth.

In India there is so much that needs to be done at an accelerated rate, especially in rural areas. All Western societies took special care of their citizens to make sure that they did not lag behind, either intellectually or materially. They provided social services and a minimum standard of living for each member of the society. Governments provide unemployment insurance for the unemployed. Those who do not qualify for unemployment insurance are given money to survive in the form of welfare. Free school education is provided for everyone with well trained teachers, free text books and other teaching aids for every student.

The government employees' expenses are too high and the country has a very large national deficit and debt. In most western countries, when the national deficit increases, government employees are laid off or their wages are cut. This did not happen in India because of the strong government employees' unions and the government's fear of creating unemployment. In China, from time to time in the last 60 years, they sent half of their government employees to villages for the uplifting of rural areas.

Government and Public Sector employee volunteers to educate / train rural people

Looking at this situation positively, the surplus of government employees can provide a great benefit to India. Our national wealth is our government employees. Almost a quarter of these employees could be given an option to work in rural areas while keeping their present job and salary. Public sector employees can be helpful in giving vocational training. In India, there are millions of unemployed people because of a lack of vocational training.

Training educated people from rural areas between the ages of 15 and 35 years would attract thousands of companies to these regions. Training would not have to be very expensive or lengthy. Training in one of the following fields, along with basic education, may be given to these people: lathe machine operator, auto mechanic, tailor, electrician, carpenter, construction worker, general repair man, leather products manufacturer (including shoes), chefs, cooks, waiters, car and truck drivers. Many factories will start coming to these rural areas because of the abundance of trained labour, following the expression, 'if you built it they will come'. Vocational training can be adjusted to the needs of a particular factory and these new industries will train their employees further in a particular skill.

Indian business men have a social responsibility towards the poor. They can donate funds, build new factories in the rural areas and can also train new employees by vocational education in rural areas. Giving their own time, in addition to money for these causes will be the biggest service they can do for India. Economic development in India has created lots of people with money. Political leaders and people in high positions can persuade others with money to generously contribute to this cause of education and training.

In rural areas, where a national telecommunication network is not available, India can skip an entire generation of technology and go wireless by installing radio towers in remote villages and wind turbines and solar (photovoltaic) power installed immediately. Currently, 350 million people do not have electricity in rural India. India can leap frog in these essential fields.

India finally has the opportunity to transform itself. Unfortunately, there are lots of hurdles on the way: the poor state of the institutions of governance, the quality of education, lack of vocational training, large population, unemployment, climate change, slums in large cities and so on. For the first time in a millennium, India has the courage to exploit this window of opportunity.

Summary

India has a long and proud history. India's recent economic performance is once again attracting world's attention. Democracy, economy, industrialization and social changes are transforming India.

India was home to one of the earliest human civilizations. The Indus Valley Civilization flourished between 3300 and 2000 BC in India.

India's top position was not limited to trade, efficiently run administration, or economics alone. Indian mathematics, astronomers, metallurgists and physicians were arguably among the best in the world and were held in high regard. Ancient India had produced a line of brilliant philosopher and mathematicians.

India invented the numerical system. Indian mathematicians made extraordinary innovations, including the concept of zero, the basis of the numerical system that we use today.

Aryabhata was able to work out that the earth is spherical and that it rotates on its axis. He even computed the circumference of the earth as 24835 miles, which is close to modern day calculation of 24900 miles.

Bhaskaracharya calculated the time taken by the earth to orbit the sun as 365.258756484 days in the 12th century. Bhaskaracharya supplied the correct answer for division by zero as well as rules for operating with irrational numbers. (If zero is divided by any number or multiplied by any number, the result is zero. If any number is divided by zero, the result is infinity.)

During the Gupta period, India became a centre for higher studies attracting scholars from all parts of India and from several foreign countries.

India has gone into decline because of its lack of cultural openness, spirit of entrepreneurship to new ideas and technologies. India did not keep up with the times.

Liberalization has clearly improved India's economic potential. The shift in 1991 was changing economic policies and all aspects of life from old inward-looking economic regime to opening out to the world. After 1991, India gradually improved its relations and trade with USA.

India is now at the crossroads. The country boasts highly competitive private companies, a booming stock market, and a modern well-disciplined financial sector. India is poised at a key moment in its history. Rapid growth is likely to continue – and even accelerate. But India cannot take its progress for granted. Public debt is high, which discourages investment in needed infrastructure.

India has not adapted the typical Asian and Chinese strategy- exporting labour-intensive, low-price manufactured goods to North America and Europe and is far behind China.

In India 70% live on less than $2 US a day, and roughly 35% of those people live on less than $1 US a day. Millions of people search for jobs outside the villages in cities, accepting any wage that is offered to them. India's rural economy is stagnant. Rural India has cheap labour ready to hire for any reason. In India, tens of millions live in slums and come from rural areas in search of jobs. What India needs is a proactive all-round development strategy and not one that happens by default.

In terms of actual US dollars, China's manufacturing industry is five times more than India's and China's export is many times more. China comes out on top in virtually every measure. China's per capita income is about four times that of India: $1,400 compared to $6,100 in China.

In India, there are millions of unemployed people because of a lack of vocational training. Currently, 350 million people do not have electricity in rural India. India can leap frog in these essential fields.

Industrial Jobs in Rural India

India At The Crossroads

Industrial Jobs in Rural India

India should invite both Public sector and private sector industries, big and medium sized -- in rural areas. These industries should add at least one project on their own, in addition to their business operations at other locations in India. Provinces or local governments should also invite Small Industries (SI) units to their rural areas, as small industries contribute to more than 40% of Indian industrial output. The aim of this project should be to create jobs in towns in the hubs of villages of these provinces and local governments.

Public Sector industries should increase presence in rural India

Until lots of private sector jobs are available in small towns of rural India, most of the public sector units should start several branches and factories throughout rural regions. Today, both public sector and private sector have become an integral part of the economy. The Indian private sector as well as the public sector has not benefited the weaker and disadvantaged sections of society especially in rural area. Jobs are not available in towns of rural areas especially in the organized sector. Both public sector and private sector should generate jobs in rural areas. Rural India needs jobs through the private sector large and small, and same with the public sector.

Liberalization and globalization has made most of the public sector industries healthy and productive. Now these public sector industries should benefit the weaker and disadvantaged sections of society by creating jobs, especially in rural India. India's centralized policy, just like the Soviet-type model that favored centralization and specialization at the country level, did not create jobs in rural towns and did not bring industry to rural towns, thereby failing to improve village life. China's view and policy of local self-sufficiency resulted in substantial decentralization and specialization at the provincial and local level. In short, India in the last 65 years has not improved the local villages, and towns, in rural areas as was done in China.

China's Township and Village Enterprises (TVEs) ultimately encouraged small cottage industries to produce goods strictly for local consumption to complex factories with foreign investment producing goods for export. The technology and industrial sector has been promoted by the government and has flourished enough to encourage foreign educated or trained Chinese managers to return home to start high-tech and manufacturing ventures. World Bank estimates show that annual growth rate of TVEs from the mid-1980s to the mid-1990s was about 25% (World Development Report, 1996). By 1995, TVEs accounted for approximately a quarter of China's GDP, two thirds of the total rural output, and more than one third of China's export earnings.

Lots of Chinese public sector units are bought by private and foreign enterprises. Now Small and medium-sized enterprises and non-public enterprises

Industrial Jobs in Rural India

have become China's main job creators. Private enterprises provide 50 percent of the employment of the entire society. China's one window quick service and inviting foreign firms by local heads or Mayors of cities [big and small] to their cities, helped develop industries. This brought in lots of foreign investment, foreign companies and technology to China. Many foreign companies bought local companies from governments and other small manufacturers. India should also follow China's example in attracting foreign capital, industry and disciplined ways of doing things. Foreign company's expenses are 10 times more than local manufacturers in the first few years of manufacturing. Reducing transaction cost is what increases the profits and makes it attractive for a manufacturing foreign company to come to a country. The transaction costs in the first few years of manufacturing are sheer losses that help no one.

More Public Sector industries needed in India

The problem which existed at the time of independence still exists in rural India today. Rapid industrialization and employment are needed. Rural India needs jobs in the private sector large and small, and same with the public sector. There is a special need for small and medium industries in rural India like the ones in China.

Many new industries can be started by private individuals (management) with local government partnership. Later they can be converted into private enterprises, as was done in China. Because of TVEs, China is years ahead and far more advanced in rural areas and townships (small cities in hubs of village clusters) than India. In light of the development of several hundred towns in the hubs of villages in China, villagers do not have to move to big cities far away from their homes. That is also a reason why China does not have slums in their big cities.

India at the time of independence had a weak industrial base, low level of savings, inadequate investments and infrastructure facilities. In view of this type of socio-economic set up, our leaders drew up a roadmap for the development of the public sector as an instrument for self-reliant economic growth, and development of core sectors through the public enterprises. The public sector did create employment in urban areas especially in big cities (or very few towns in the midst of the villages). The same type of situation (unemployment, lack of training, and absence of industry) now exists in villages or towns in the hubs of villages 64 years after independence.

When the country became independent the industrial sector accounted for 13% of the economy (Gross Domestic Products). Thanks to heavy public-sector investment, the share of industry grew steadily through the fifties, sixties and seventies. By the end of the seventies the share of industry had increased to 23%. By 2007, the share of industry stood at 26% of GDP. The share of the industrial sector is barely larger than what it was quarter century ago. In China industrial and construction sectors now account for 58% of its GDP.

Public Sector is very healthy now

With the advent of globalization, the public sector faced new challenges in the developing of economies. The public sector enterprises now have to face healthy competition both from domestic and international competitors. Global competition has ended Indian public sector monopoly and improved its financial condition. The public sector and the private sector now have a chance to improve the life and condition of almost half a billion people. These public sector enterprises should not only multiply their branches but also add other sectors in their manufacturing. Public sector enterprises have now accumulated all the expertise, finances and credibility to get money from the banks.

> "Many companies in the public sector have proved themselves to be wealth creators and profit generators. In recent times, the credible performance of public companies in the stock market shows the public confidence in them. Some have also emerged as effective players in the international markets. The 2009 Forbes list of 2000 companies includes 47 Indian companies. Among these, 25 were Indian public sector companies."

President of India, Pratibha Patil (New Delhi, April 10, 2010).

In 2006-07, there were 247 Central Public Sector Enterprises in India. They have accumulated a large amount of Reserves and Surplus which stood at Rs. 416494 crores as on March 31, 2007. High profits were reported by companies under the cognate groups of Petroleum (Rs.33,442 crore), Telecommunications Services (Rs.14,126 crore), Power Generation (12,115 crore), Coal and Lignite (Rs.8,853 crore), Steel (Rs.7,612 crore), Minerals & Metals (Rs. 5246 crore), Financial Services (Rs.2,828), Transportation services (Rs.2,210 crore) and Heavy Engineering (Rs. 2,123 crore).

(Source – Public Enterprises- Annual survey of CPSEs – 2006-07)

During the period since 1991, successive governments have carried forward the country's economic reforms in Industrial, Trade and Financial sectors.

New Opportunities for public sector to grow

Acquisitions, joint ventures and green field projects in Petroleum Sector have already taken place and are under active consideration in Power, Coal and Mining sectors. Public sector companies and nationalized banks should be encouraged to enter the capital market to raise resources and offer new investment avenues to industries and retail investors.

All these nationalized banks plus all the other banks and financial companies should coordinate their

Industrial Jobs in Rural India

efforts to have branches covering all the rural areas of India. These financial institutions should have very innovative ways to do business in rural areas. They should send out loan officers or bank representatives to the surrounding villages to sanction or approve loans. A very big percentage of their resources should be invested as loans in rural areas. Giving loans to industries, other businesses and micro loans to individuals or mini businesses for the development of rural regions should be encouraged.

Bharat Heavy Electricals, Rural Electrification corpn, Power Grid corpn, Steel Authority of India, Gail (India), Bharat Electronics, Gujarat Mineral Devp., Corpn., IFCI, BEML, HMT, Engineers India, are either in alternative source of energy field or can have collaboration with other countries to develop the biggest future industry of alternative sources of energy. All the public sector industries should double or triple their manufacturing facilities and spread especially in small towns in the hubs of village groupings throughout India.

India has such great brainpower in both the public and private sectors. This should be exploited to make India's industrial hubs. Job growth is only possible in all these public undertakings with diversified manufacturing. They all should have multiple portfolios operating at the same time. Apart from the main one, they should have presence in many industry segments. So that even if one portfolio goes down, the others take care of the downside.

Successful Indian Public Sector Industries

Bharat Heavy Electricals Ltd (BHEL) is one of the largest engineering and manufacturing enterprises in the world. Since its inception 45 Years back, BHEL has been at the helm of ushering in the indigenous heavy electrical equipment industry in India. It manufactures over 180 products under 30 product groups and caters to sectors like power generation and transmission, industry, transportation, telecommunication and renewable energy. The company has been growing at an impressive rate of 30%over the past few years. This growth has been made possible primarily due to its diversified and multiple portfolios of businesses.

Oil and Natural Gas Corporation Limited (ONGC) is an Indian public sector oil and gas company. Indian government holds 74.14% equity stake in this company. It is a Fortune Global 500 company ranked 152nd, and contributes 77% of India's crude oil production and 81% of India's natural gas production. It is the highest profit making corporation in India. It produces about 30% of India's crude oil requirement. Most of the oil companies in the western world are investing a lot of money in renewable energy. The same type of investment by all the Indian oil companies should be done in renewable energy field in India.

National Thermal Power Corporation (NTPC) is the largest power generation company in *India.* Most of the thermal power corporations in the western world are investing a lot of money in renewable energy. All the Indian thermal companies should invest in renewable energy.

Steel Authority of India Limited (SAIL), a Navratna company, is one of the largest steel makers in India. The company is among the top five highest profit earning corporates of the country. It is a public sector undertaking which trades publicly in the market, is wholly owned by Government of India and acts like an operating company. SAIL is the 16th largest steel producer in the world. According to a recent survey, SAIL is one of India's fastest growing Public Sector Units.

Since its inception, Power Finance Corporation (PFC) has been providing financial assistance to power projects across India including generation, transmission and distribution. To increase the business in renewables, co-generation, energy saving projects and captive power plants, PFC has selected a list of 31 business development associates. It has also signed an agreement with Gujarat Energy Development Agency for development of renewable energy generation projects. In 2008-09, it had sanctioned Rs 560 crore for projects in the sector.

National Mineral Development Corporation (NMDC) is a Public Sector Enterprise under the Ministry of Steel, Government of India and a multi-locational, multi product and consistently profit making organization with large turnover is in the process of massive expansion and diversification activities both in India and abroad. NMDC is entering into new area of Wind Energy.

Demographic changes and literacy

Demographic changes could have positive effects on India. The country's large and growing population has been a problem in the past. India's efforts to stabilize the population were not as effective as the Chinese 'One child policy.' Demographic shift and education have a huge impact on economic performance, as younger workers are more energetic and more open to new technology.

India's hope for a big payoff from population growth ignores where people are living. Rising population helps drive growth with education and vocational training. When people are moving to higher-paying and more productive factory jobs in the cities and not surviving in depressed condition in farm regions. If working-age people can be productively employed, India's economic growth stands to accelerate. Failure to take advantage of the opportunities inherent in demographic change can lead to economic stagnation. India's demographic profile should be used to favor economic growth.

Domestic savings for new industries will increase significantly. Increased savings raises the investment rate and this in turn generates employment for the expanding labor force. Employment growth generates income that then further boosts savings.

These circumstances were very similar to what existed in other Asian countries at the time of 'take-off'. China entered the demographic phase in the late eighties with a literacy rate of around 80%. Within a generation, the process created infrastructure, industrial capacity and raised living standards.

Over the next few years, India will see both a sharp increase in literacy rates and there will be a large percentage of working age people. These conditions can deliver very rapid growth to an underdeveloped economy (similar to India) and upgrade standards of living at a very fast pace.

Infrastructure and new imported technologies can deliver very rapid growth to an underdeveloped economy and upgrade the standard of living. Medium and low technology manufacturing is an area that can benefit from the availability of cheap capital and labor. India will now copy China and begin building massive factories, employing tens of thousands of workers. India should not shy away from taking advantage of this opportunity. India needs to upgrade technology and be better educated about technology. One just has to observe, learn and adopt as Japan, China and other Southeast Asian countries did.

Present condition in India -- and need for job creation

Some new towns or cities should be seeded in the hubs

of rural areas. With modern technology, it is possible to have a number of decentralized industries in the rural regions. These industries would maintain world-class levels and become part of a globally competitive industry.

Many agro industries, services industries and even high tech concerns can be relocated in such new cities by moving a few government offices and providing special concessions for industries. Once the process of value-adding agro-food industry starts, economic activities will be generated in a big way.

Industry and trade are the best guarantees for development, prosperity and job creation. Industry and trade drive the world's economy as well as a nation's economy. The more a country trades and has industries in hubs of villages or mini-new cities close to villages, the more prosperous it will become. Public and private sector industries should be encouraged to move to the rural towns in the hubs of the village groupings.

New Towns needed in village cluster group hubs

The central government should encourage labor intensive industries in new cities in the hubs of rural areas or Special Economic Zones (SEZ). Public and private investments are required in such areas with roads, irrigation works, solar power, tourism, textile industry, and railways. Railways and advanced textile industries, and other key industries should be expanded and modernized.

It should be noted that no country has achieved growth and prosperity through a village-based model of development. This is why India requires small new towns and mini-cities in the middle of the village or hubs of village clusters. China, which in many ways resembles India, abandoned the village-based model of development long ago and developed hundreds of mini-new cities or towns in the hubs of villages. Tens of thousands of industries were built in the hubs of villages or in mini-new cities in China and hundreds of millions of jobs were generated for the unemployed and under employed people.

In China the manufacturing sector, especially in new cities, has absorbed hundreds of millions of people coming out of rural areas. In India this economy of scale will work in mini-new cities as well. India has about 70% or 900 million people spread over 600,000 villages. Clearly there is no need to urbanize all the villages, however mini-new cities in the hubs of the villages are the best alternative.

Banks are flushed with money and this money should be channeled into manufacturing, business and agriculture in the rural areas. Agriculture, small businesses and small industries need micro loans from the banks and other sources. Even large industries and big businesses in these remote areas will need large bank loans.

India should have a job creation policy for the less educated and uneducated young men and women in rural areas. The unemployed workforce lives largely in rural regions. In despair they will migrate to the cities, adding to the woes of urban areas. Every irrigation project must be given funds to be completed in double-quick time.

India needs to implement massive irrigation and road-building projects. Improvements to railways should be made, including in rural areas. Railways should lay more rail lines in these poor regions.

India needs to create rural business hubs using the Chinese model. India should also follow China's example in attracting foreign capital, industry and disciplined ways of doing things. Its economic output will grow to $4 trillion (U.S.) by 2020, from 1.6 trillion today and its output per capita, a more accurate measure of wealth, will triple to $3,000 per person.

India's manufacturing sector has to be one of the biggest drivers for growth. Over the coming years, this sector needs to absorb the tens of millions of people coming out of rural India. The manufacturing sector and service sector will go hand in hand.

Township and village Enterprises (TVEs in rural China)

China's successful development and employment for all, is because of industry developed in rural China. From the very beginning the Chinese have tried to improve their village life. In spite of their best efforts, it took some time to be successful in villages, to modernize agriculture and non-agricultural products. The rural enterprises first appeared in the 1950s, but it was only in the Deng Xiaoping era that they multiplied. After reform, commune owned enterprises were reclassified as Township and Village Enterprises (TVEs).

The implicit contract between the township and village governments in the rural areas and the TVEs led to cooperation and efficiency. The capital invested in TVEs originated from local sources and by massive loans from the state banking system. Township-village Governments (TVGs) are part of a large government system with broad powers. Often, they act as guarantors for TVEs (investment loans given by the banks).

The key factor for TVE success is that the capital invested in TVEs originated from local sources. The close relationship between banks and local governments often helped TVEs. Because of government support, banks also favored lending to TVEs. It is relatively easier for collective TVEs to obtain loans than private enterprises, since collective TVEs have the community government backing them up.

Hundreds of new towns and small cities were established with these TVEs. These TVEs exploited the resources of the country to become successful manufacturing companies. Support from local level and province was guaranteed to TVEs as they were often the single most important source of local government's revenue. Recently, employment grew significantly in the industry field, as more and more

TVEs converted from public to private sector industries. Many provinces' employment of the rural workforce grew from 40% to 50%.

TVEs were very flexible in terms of organizational structure. TVE sector experienced dramatic changes in 1995-1996. After the mid-1990s, TVEs were forced to restructure substantially with increased market integration and competition. The greater push towards a free market enterprise, accomplished the transitory or temporary role of most TVEs. The changes in the economic environment gradually reduced the benefits of public ownership. The creation of TVEs worked out to a large extent as China's transition strategy.

This also encouraged small cottage industries producing goods for strictly local consumption to complex factories with foreign investment, producing goods for export. The technology and industrial sector has been promoted by the government and flourished enough to encourage foreign educated or trained Chinese managers to return home to start high-tech and manufacturing ventures. In China, by and large, the expatriate has played a much bigger role. In 1978, China did not have the internal markets to rely on, so they turned to the overseas Chinese, because they were the only people who could understand China well. To other people China seemed too difficult, too alien, too foreign. China has embraced its non-resident, While India has shunned it.

Government owned Industry of China

Industrial Jobs in Rural India

China is tremendously successful because of its policy of multiplying success. When they establish one factory of a kind, after its success, they multiply the same success formula ten times, every time improving on the previous one. Creating employment is their main objective. Many government factories are making a lot of money with a joint venture with foreign partners. Big acquisitions by Chinese businesses include Lenovo's takeover of IBM's PC business and more recently the Chinese acquisition of an interest in Blackstone.

In terms of manufacturing, China's lead over India is considerable. China is the world's second largest nation in terms of manufacturing, after the U.S. India's manufacturing is impressive, but much further back, in 12th place. As can be seen, China is by far the bigger economy, the bigger exporter and the bigger importer. In terms of jobs, China has produced jobs several times more than India, especially in rural towns, which have already grown to become big cities.

China's cotton textile industry is the largest in the world. The industry is labor-intensive and played a prominent role in the industrial boom of the late 1980s and early 1990s. In addition to garments and textiles, output from light industry includes footwear, toys, food processing, and consumer electronics. This is a big export earner for China and a very large creator of jobs.

High technology industries produce high-speed computers, 600 types of semiconductors, specialized electronic telecommunications equipment.

Machinery and transportation equipment have been the mainstay of Chinese exports. They comprised China's leading export sector for a successive 11 years from 1996 to 2006.

Thermal, hydro and nuclear power industries are the fastest growing of all industrial sectors. Power grid construction has entered its fastest ever development; main power grids now cover all the cities and most rural areas.

China is developing new energy resources, such as wind, solar, geothermal, and tidal power. Its abundant wind energy resources give China the potential for mass-produced wind power. Between 2001 and 2005, the government invested 1.5 billion yuan in the wind power industry. Given northern China's rich wind energy resources, its wind power industry has attracted domestic and overseas investment -- and establishment of Asia's largest wind power station, with an investment of 10 billion yuan and a capacity of one million kw.

China's automobile production is projected to reach 9.4 million, and the country could become the number-one automaker in the world by 2020. By 2004 China had become the world's fourth largest automotive vehicle manufacturer.

Summary

India needs expansion of public sector industries in addition to private sector industries to provide jobs especially in rural areas. The Indian industrial sector is very small compared to the Chinese industrial sector.

The public and private sectors are integral parts of the Indian economy. But, private sector industry cannot be expected to start industry in rural areas for the sake of job creation while public sector should. Private sector industries will soon find that it is to their advantage to start branches of their business in mini-new cities.

Chinese small and medium industry got a lot of help from provincial or local governments when they started as Township and Village Enterprises (TVEs) in the public sector and later on many of them were converted into private sector ventures.

From the very beginning, Chinese have tried to improve their village life. Because of government support banks also favoured lending to TVEs in China. Thousands of new towns and small cities were established with the TVEs. These TVEs exploited the resources of the country to become successful manufacturing companies.

The creation of TVEs worked out to a large extent China's transition strategy. TVEs also encouraged small cottage industry in China producing goods for

India At The Crossroads

strictly local consumption to complex factories with foreign investment producing goods for export.

In India multinational (foreign) companies sell only to rich and middle class people. These companies look to sell to 300 million people in India as compared to China, a billion people plus (is) a very big export market. These companies (and other local companies) find the Indian local markets more lucrative and sell their manufactured goods at much higher prices to them. The export market is not attractive to them, where they export from China only. In China a very large number of local manufacturing companies have come up, with foreign technology they have created competition for multinationals. With WTO compulsions (facilities), Chinese companies not only sell to the West, but are increasingly exporting cheap manufactured goods to India. Multinational companies also export manufactured goods to India from China instead of manufacturing in India.

India's public sector is very healthy now. With foreign collaboration, Public sector companies should multiply production of their manufactured goods. There are many areas where goods like computer hardware can be manufactured. Previously most of the employees in these public sector undertakings benefited. Now the same benefits can be spread over to the people of new towns in the hubs of village clusters. This will create jobs in small towns and lift the economy of the region.

Can India see itself as the Next China?

India At The Crossroads

Can India see itself as the Next China?

It is only in the last decade that India came to see itself economically as the next China and its growing population as a competitive advantage rather than a threat. The recent case of national overconfidence could give way just as fast to a healthier sense of urgency, with new leaders working on improving job opportunities and education.

Demographic dividend advocates are ignoring the huge challenge of educating all the young people and expanding the job opportunities available to the ten million entering the labour force every year. Population growth can be huge advantage only if a nation works hard to set young workers for productive careers.

A recent survey by the consulting firm Aon Hewitt shows that salaries of urban workers (organized sector) in India are rising faster than anywhere else in Asia, with average wages increasing by nearly 13 percent in 2011 – a symptom of the fact that when so few workers are highly skilled, those who are can charge a premium. Unfortunately, only ten per cent people of India are employed in organized sector.

Indian high wages are due to its staff union demands in urban areas. Through collective bargaining, they have managed to raise their wages. Meanwhile, a large number of people in rural India are unemployed and starving. The industrial sector in India is highly unionized, and these unions are preventing absorption of labour by keeping industrial wages at an artificially high level. In today's globally integrated world, production can move swiftly to the lower-cost factories, to the cheaper labour markets – to countries like Indonesia and Bangladesh.

Indian high wages are discouraging new factories to come up. Employed people in government and in private sector are getting more money and more benefits, while others (workers) remain under employed or unemployed. All policy makers and the democratic systems, support employed and organized workers. Policy makers have no time for unemployed and invisible people.

Indian government expenses, government service wages and pensions increased considerably in the last two decades. The Government's excessive spending may set off hyperinflation and may crowd out private investment, ending the country's boom. This may also trigger a wage-price spiral.

In the book "Breakout Nations" Ruchir Sharma, a large investor in emerging markets for Morgan Stanley, identifies countries that are most likely to leap ahead and why. In the book, he writes:

> India's confidence ignored the postwar experience of many countries in Africa and the Middle East, where a flood of young people (getting) into the labour market produced unemployment, unrest, and more mouths to feed. The conventional view is that India will be able to put all those people to work -- because of its relatively strong education system, entrepreneurial zeal, and strong links to global economy. All of that is real, but India

Can India see itself as the Next China?

is already showing some of the warning signs of failed growth stories, including early-onset overconfidence. Many outsiders were just as confident before the recent sign of trouble. I put the probability of India's continuing its journey as a breakout nation this decade at close to 50 percent, owing to a whole series of risks that the Indian and foreign elites leave out of the picture, including bloated government, crony capitalism, falling turnover among the rich and powerful, and a disturbing tendency of farmers to stay on the farm. (Page 38)

No other large economy has so many stars aligned in its favor, from its demographic profile to its entrepreneurial energy and perhaps most important, an annual per capita income that is only one-fourth of China's. But destiny can never be taken for granted. Indian policy makers cannot assume that demographics will triumph and that problems such as rising crony capitalism and increased welfare spending are just sideshows instead of major challenges. These are exactly the factors that have prematurely choked growth in other emerging markets. (page 58)

India's policy of large debt and deficit will be a big problem. For the last five years, government spending has been growing at 20 percent annual rate; much faster than the economy. Over these five years, India's total fiscal deficit has increased from 6 percent to 9 percent of GDP. The total debt has increased. The total public-debt-to-GDP ratio is now 70 percent -- among the highest for any major developing country.

The problems of debt, corruption, population and unemployment have not been the highest priority to India's policy makers. Indian policy makers cannot assume that demographics will triumph. They, until recently, were very confident that the country would become the fastest-growing major economy this decade. The positive view is that even with these problems, India may still progress. India still has plenty of room to grow from a low base of per capita income of US $1,400.

It takes money, both in domestic savings and foreign investment to grow. But for nations to grow rapidly it is much easier to be poor – the poorer, the better. India still has plenty of potential to grow from a low base, India with ($1,400 per capita income, with a high growth population) and China ($6,000 per capita income, with a shrinking population). The richer the country, the tougher the growth challenges. In the early stages of development, emerging nations can narrow the income gap with rich nations with relative ease, by borrowing or copying the technology and management tools of cutting-edge nations.

Yet, history suggests that in economic development, there is no straight path to the top. There is a huge pool of competitors. And only a few nations defy the long odds against success. The growth game is all about beating expectations – your peers and rivals.

The China slowdown will not come fast and hard

Can India see itself as the Next China?

The slowdown in China will not come fast and hard. They will keep their export momentum going, adding many more new destination markets. Their internal consumption will increase. They will have full employment for many years to come. China still has plenty of space to grow, though at a slower rate. Income and standard of living of their masses will rise considerably. The Chinese economy is now very large -- and worth around $6 trillion a year – that even with 6 percent growth rate, will remain the largest single contributor to global growth in the coming years. China will be doing well in the healthy middle-income sector both with domestic consumption and export.

China can continue to grow by changing its focus to domestic consumption and slower export growth pace. China's prices for export and local consumption are still lower compared to India's. In China, tens of millions of rural Chinese will migrate to the cities over the next two decades -- as they have done in the last two. The sheer scale and scope of urbanization in China is staggering. By 2020, the urban population is expected to increase from 46 to 60 percent, equivalent to tens of millions of new urban residents and hundreds of new satellite cities.

China was able to convert its growing labour force into an economic miracle by encouraging farmers to move to the higher paying and more productive factory jobs in the new cities. The Chinese created hundreds of new cities and their urban population rose much faster than India's. Over the past decade, the share of the Chinese population living in urban areas rose from 35 to 46 percent. During the same period India's urban population grew more slowly – from 26 percent to 30 percent.

The most important factor behind the boom of emerging markets was worldwide flood of easy money. Private capital flow into developing countries has surged from an annual pace of $200 Billion in 2000 to nearly a trillion dollars a year in 2010. China took advantage of cheap capital. China opened doors to foreign capital, particularly when the capital came with technology and market as part of the bargain. Also, to create jobs, Beijing ordered banks to open the tap on loans fully for public sector and private sector industries. They (banks) have now slowed down the lending – after China reached almost full employment.

To create jobs, Indian government should also instruct its nationalized banks to open the tap for loans generously, for public sector and private sector industries, especially in rural areas -- India should also open doors to foreign capital, particularly when the capital comes with technology, industry and markets as part of the bargain. India's aim should be to increase employment in organized sector to 25 percent instead of current ten per cent. Industries will increase in rural India as the expenses and wages in rural locations may be much less compared to urban sites.

China now sits on $2.5 trillion in foreign-currency reserves, and is a major creditor to the United States. In the next 10 to 15 years, China may double its foreign-currency reserves – say to $5 trillion. China will be a major creditor not only to United States but to the rest of the world including India. On the other hand, India's growth has slowed and imports are increasing faster than its exports.

Rationing & Chinese rural industrialization strategy that India could emulate!

China's rural labor market and employment structure have changed dramatically in the last 25 years – as millions of rural workers found non-farm employment. China's official statistics indicate that the number of rural workers with non-farm occupations in local rural enterprises rose from 67 million in 1985 to 127 million in 1999. The share rose from 18 to 28 per cent in that period. In the 15 years between 1980 and 1994, the number of rural enterprises had grown 16.5 times.

Rationing of industrial jobs was used in the initial stages of industrial development in China. One form of implementation was Time Rationing, under which people's industrial working days were limited. This form of Time rationing was caused by the pressure from local authorities to maximize employment.

The unique feature of rationing jobs in India is to allowing job sharing among people in the same local community, a practice that is widely observed in Chinese state-owned enterprises. When industrial jobs are limited, rationing could be an effective way to balance income distribution in an impoverished community.

The reason for implementing job rationing was shortage of industrial jobs in rural China. Job rationing became necessary to make jobs available to those who did not have regular work. In China Job rationing was the controlled distribution of the scarce resources – industrial jobs and services in rural areas. As industrial jobs became more readily available, there was no need for job rationing.

In China, local governments aimed at creating more employment and reducing individual working days in the industrial sector. Workers in rural regions worked 167 days less than those in urban areas.

There are some similarities in China's rationed rural industrial jobs and Indian NREGA (National Rural Employment Guarantee Act). Chinese industrial jobs pay much more than Indian NREGA. It is not limited to one job per family, 100 work days a year, only agricultural work and limited funds, and the government providing jobs to all rural workers.

Although the Indian rationing of rural (as proposed) industrial jobs and their duration may be 150 to 200 days a year, they may pay much more than Indian government sponsored NREGA. The rationing of industrial jobs in the initial stages of Indian rural development will bring prosperity to hundreds of millions of people.

Pressure from the local authorities to maximize employment is missing in India, as is industrialization in rural areas. India's rural residents should have the opportunity to take industrial jobs – more industrial

Can India see itself as the Next China?

jobs should be made available in the *'kasbahs'* and village clusters of India.

Some kind of rationing of industrial jobs is needed in rural locations. Rationing is not a new concept in India. People were used to food, kerosene oil, coal and cloth rationing in British colonial India during the World War II years, when they were in short supply. As industrial jobs become more available, there will be no need for rationing of jobs, as was discontinued when food, fuel and clothing were no longer in short supply.

Food rationing was introduced in the United States in the 1940's, during the crisis of World War II. In India, rather than food crisis there is job crisis. Every day 3,000 children are dying due to mal-nutrition because their families do not have adequate income. This number does not include adults who are dying for the same reason.

India should overhaul its labour laws

Many experts say India, already attractive for its cheap labour and its engineering skills, could bring in even more foreign companies if it could free its labour market of red tape. India is still far from creating mass jobs in large-scale manufacturing.

There is a need for labour market reform. India has one of the most restrictive labour law systems in the world with respect to worker dismissal, a feature that over the past two decades has prompted manufacturing businesses to hire more casual workers. Many times even dismissal of temporary or casual workers is a problem. Shrinking organised employment is the consequence of these policies.

Labour market reform is essential if firms are to retain their competitiveness, and in some instances simply survive the dynamics of global business. It should be possible for Indian firms, workers and policy makers to devise creative solutions to overcome India's own specific rigidities.

The Factory Act of 1948 is the fundamental labour law in the organized sector and is mandated for all factories. It aims to regulate working conditions in factories. The net effect of these acts (and amendments) is that effective mechanisms for employers to flexibly adjust labour requirements to changing technological or market conditions is lacking. These acts have led to economic inefficiencies in a number of ways. India's labour market is ranked 45th for degree of labour market flexibility in the Global Competitiveness Report (GCR) 1998.

In India firms employing more than 100 workers must seek government permission for any retrenchments they wish to make, and the workers in these firms are entitled to three months notice for any such action. As for plant closings, companies employing more than 100 workers must receive government permission before any closure; the government may grant or deny permission for such a closing, even if the company is losing money on the operation. This process of government permission could take years.

When companies encounter adverse business conditions, the retrenchment legislation compels them to maintain bloated work forces, leaving fewer resources for investment in new production processes and lines of activity.

With greater openness to international trade, India's labour-intensive manufactures and exports could expand. The post-reform period witnessed a significant improvement in wages. One reason for this could be the rigidities in labour markets — impeding mobility of labour to expanding sectors. There is a need for labour market reforms that could overcome some of the existing rigidities.

Anti-retrenchment legislation may have even more paradoxical effects. Because the legislation raises labour costs, companies may hire fewer workers than they might otherwise have, and they may not enter a particular product line in the first place. These consequences of the legislation is ironic because it suggests that, in terms of overall impact, this seemingly protective law may actually be harming labourers rather than helping them.

Many observers have claimed that India's protective labour legislation has hurt India's overall growth. In most cases labour legislation may have actually hurt

India At The Crossroads

the labour it was meant to protect (unemployed rural labour). The rigid retrenchment laws increased the costs of adjusting a firm's employment level and led firms to consider not only current market conditions, but also future labour needs while making their labour decisions. A firm will therefore be reluctant to hire additional workers during an economic upturn — if it anticipates significant costs in reducing its work force during a subsequent downturn. This has hurt employment situation in India. By not increasing labour intensive industries which are badly needed.

Only about 10 percent of India's workforce is in the organized sector. Organized sector labour, which is highly unionized, has managed to achieve significant growth in real wages, much ahead of the growth of per capita income in the country's economy. Large industries managed to absorb these higher wages, because the markets were protected from world competition through trade restrictions — and the firms could pass on the higher costs to consumers.

While India is a labour surplus economy, wages are often set at above market clearing levels, especially in the organized sector. Government's employees are mostly unionized, assured of lifetime employment, and face very little risk of being fired.

If India overhauls its labour laws, its manufacturing export could grow five to ten times more. That means providing jobs to almost all, by encouraging and increasing foreign companies, besides Indian public and private industries in rural India.

Can India see itself as the Next China?

The problem is becoming even more pressing — as India competes with China. Employees in China, often work 12 hours a day (in the initial stages); in India eight. Chinese workers get two days of vacation a month, compared four in India. Many specialists agree that economic future of India is at stake.

China is a manufacturing and export phenomenon. The question is often asked: when the economic rivalry between the two emerging economic powers China and India will intensify? Both societies have enormous populations and need to absorb 10 million to 15 million new workers each year. In the years ahead, both countries are going to be competing for manufacturing jobs. China's embrace of market capitalism married to focused, powerful and centralized government — gives it an edge.

Every global company wants to hedge against political risks by spreading its manufacturing centers across geographic boundaries. Thus, even if China dominates, India will be able to get its share of manufacturing contracts. More over when you look at market economies, the richer countries are democracies.

India's labour unrest and its trade union militancy serve as a reminder that India has far to go before it stands alongside the world's other economic powerhouses. But first, it must show it can ride out booms and slowdowns alike. Executives and industry groups say relaxing the labour laws would allow companies to hire more workers and attract more manufacturers to India.

Labour laws at present "really hurt the interests of labour (unemployed rural labour) more than any other category," said Kaushik Basu, the chief economic adviser at the finance ministry.

In rural India, hundreds of millions of industrial jobs could be created. These jobs may be temporary in nature. Rural workers should have an option to work — say 200 days a year in industry and 150 days in the fields (agriculture). There can be a rationing of industrial jobs in rural India, as is done in China.

A demographically young India will be the largest contributor to the global labour force in the coming decades, and will add about 110 million workers by 2020. To be able to reap dividends from favorable demographics, India will have to overhaul its labour laws that restrict hire-and-fire policies — and invest heavily in education and skills training. There should be special laws for the poor and backward rural areas — where the unemployment situation is alarming — until India attains full employment and twenty five percent of the employed work force is deployed in the organized sector.

India can boast of a quarter of the world's workforce by 2025, provided the country harnesses the potential of its young and productive population. But the demographic dividend would become a disaster if India does not radically overhaul the labour ecosystem to enhance the productivity of the growing workforce. If reforms are not initiated, it is likely that much of the country's demographic dividend would occur in states with backward labour market ecosystems with education and training, infrastructure, governance.

The trade unions have conducted several mass agitations opposing the reform initiatives and policies in the form of all-India strikes, *morchas* (processions) and *dharnas* (sit-ins), to protest against the reform proposals. Trade unions have built alliances with new forms of workers' organizations, non-governmental organizations (NGOs) and other social organizations to build mass movements.

Several state governments have liberalized regulations and changed the labour administrative framework with respect to establishments in the Special Economic Zones. The self-certification system has been introduced in many SEZs in India. The units in the SEZs are declared under the Industrial Development Act as "public utility services" which render strikes difficult — if not impossible. There have been amendments to other aspects of labour laws like minimum wages, safety and health, hire and fire rights. All taken together, affect the labour market, governance of units and labour rights of workers in the SEZs.

In this age of globalization, the employment structure across the globe has been undergoing changes in all nations. In order to effectively compete in a globalized market, one needs flexibility relating to labour, capital, or bureaucracy. This allows a producer to adapt to the fast - changing world and compete effectively. In particular, it is argued that stringent labour regulations not only put domestic producers at a disadvantage — but also deter foreign direct investment — and eventually impact adversely on investment, output and employment. Over the last two decades, a number of countries have attempted to liberalize their labour markets and have also amended their labour laws to make them more investment and employment friendly.

Invite multinational companies ... to improve job prospects

In China, initial transition costs were eliminated to attract multinational companies. Many of these incoming companies bought parts of the Chinese Public sector industries or TVEs (Township and Village Enterprises). They came with capital, technology and markets. These foreign companies are now exporting to the USA and other western country destinations from China.

In India, many public sector companies should become more flexible in terms of organizational structure and regulations as done in China. The other option is that some of these public sector companies can have joint ventures with multinationals. India could identify, approach – and select multinational companies that suit its needs. These companies should be selected on the basis of export potential, import substitution and local consumer demand projections.

Ground work should be laid by Indian Public or Private sector companies – so that the multinational ventures do not waste time nor lose money in the initial stages of business (reduce transaction cost) start up. These multinational companies should be able to buy part of public or private sector industries. They should be able to start manufacturing in India immediately on plant installation, so that they do not lose millions of dollars. The incoming companies should have the option of joint ventures or acquiring part of Public Sector Companies without losing money in initial stages of business. The Indian Public sector industry should be ready with flexible organizational structure. They should be ready with land, licenses if required, operational factories with some labor and management.

Many multinational companies may come to India. In addition to other advantages Uttar Pradesh, Bihar, Madhya Pradesh, and Odisha still have abundance of available (unemployed) and cheap labor. Places like (eastern) UP, Bihar and Madhya Pradesh should develop new towns in the hubs of village clusters. The seed money could come from the Central government – leaving rest of the development to the private sector. They should invite public, private and multinational manufacturing companies as stake holders, to these new towns. They should have all weather roads, hotels, airports, container parks, 'dry ports' on the outskirts of these new towns.

In Odisha, dry ports for import and export should be connected to Paradip sea port by fast freight trains and good highways. A 'dry port' is an inland cargo terminal directly connected by road or rail to a sea port. It needs to have all the facilities offered by sea ports, including storage warehouses and customs clearance services. It is important to create new seaports in Odisha or West Bengal to relieve work load and congestion of ships waiting for berths at the country's existing harbor facilities. Such dedicated sea ports will considerably increase export from Uttar Pradesh, Bihar, Madhya Pradesh, Jharkhand, Chhattisgarh and Odisha.

To avoid multiplicity and overlap of controls and clearances, Special Economic Zones (SEZ) should be established in these areas. As operational in the vicinity of the newer sea ports in India – these special economic zones will help bring in world-class infrastructure to these unstable fiscal regimes. This will also attract large, foreign investments – with technology and markets, to India. An Administrator should be appointed at such new towns to coordinate the activities of Central, State and Municipal administrations. All the multinational, public and private sector companies should be encouraged to have an apprenticeship program. This way, the business and industry receive low cost manpower for two to four years, while the youths learn a new trade, both on-the-job as well as, studying theory (at the vocational training institute or with these industries).

Apprenticeship programs with vocational training are very popular in Germany, where youths work as apprentices for three to four years. Youths in Russia and the newly independent former Soviet Union countries in eastern Europe and Central Asia opt for vocational training – where they work part time (at minimum wages), as apprentices with industry for two to four years and study simultaneously – vocational training institutes, for acquiring a firm grounding on the theory. In China too, there is a very good apprenticeship program. Chinese skilled workers are available in abundance, which is attracting capital and industry from all over the world.

Under the Russian school education system – still followed in all 14 countries of the erstwhile Soviet Union – boys are taught the use of basic tools for carpentry, electrical circuits at home, handling plumbing emergencies and maintenance of two wheeler vehicles. By the time of school leaving, youths try to own a tools kit. They are considered eligible recruits for automobile and farm equipment servicing workshop internships. They are readily inducted for two years of national service in the military, where they are given opportunities to gain more skills in using their hands effectively. The work force that emerges will find jobs easily.

Multinational companies will pour billions of dollars into the Indian economy, provided they are welcomed into India (the same way as China does). They will take advantage of the country's cheap and available labor and potentially the world's huge market.

Summary

China can continue to grow by changing its focus to domestic consumption and slower export growth pace. China's prices for export and local consumption are still lower compared to India's.

Indian government expenses, government service wages and pensions increased considerably in the last two decades. The Government's excessive spending may set off hyperinflation and may crowd out private investment, ending the country's boom. This may also trigger a wage-price spiral.

India's policy of large debt and deficit will be a big problem. For the last five years, government spending has been growing at 20 percent annual rate; much faster than the economy. The problems of debt, corruption, population and unemployment have not been the highest priority to India's policy makers. History suggests that in economic development, there is no straight path to the top. The growth game is all about beating expectations – your peers and rivals.

China was able to convert its growing labour force into an economic miracle by encouraging farmers to move to the higher paying and more productive factory jobs in the new cities. The Chinese created hundreds of new cities and their urban population rose much faster than India's.

Can India see itself as the Next China?

China now sits on $2.5 trillion in foreign-currency reserves, and is a major creditor to the United States. China will be a major creditor not only to United States but to the rest of the world including India. On the other hand, India's growth has slowed and imports are increasing faster than its exports.

Rationing of industrial jobs was used in the initial stages of industrial development in China. One form of implementation was Time Rationing, under which people's industrial working days were limited. This form of Time rationing was caused by the pressure from local authorities to maximize employment.

Although the Indian rationing of rural (as proposed) industrial jobs and their duration may be 150 to 200 days a year, they may pay much more than Indian government sponsored NREGA. The rationing of industrial jobs in the initial stages of Indian rural development will bring prosperity to hundreds of millions of people.

India should overhaul its labour laws. Many experts say India, already attractive for its cheap labour and its engineering skills, could bring in even more foreign companies if it could free its labour market of red tape. India is still far from creating mass jobs in large-scale manufacturing.

There is a need for labour market reform. India has one of the most restrictive labour law systems in the world with respect to worker dismissal. Many times even dismissal of temporary or casual workers is a problem. Shrinking organised employment is the consequence of these policies.

Labour market reform is essential if firms are to retain their competitiveness. In India firms employing more than 100 workers must seek government permission for any retrenchments they wish to make. The government may grant or deny permission for such a closing, even if, the company is losing money on the operation. This process of government permission could take years.

When companies encounter adverse business conditions, the retrenchment legislation compels them to maintain bloated work forces, leaving fewer resources for investment in new production processes and lines of activity.

While India is a labour surplus economy, wages are often set at above market clearing levels, especially in the organized sector. The problem is becoming even more pressing — as India competes with China. Many specialists agree that economic future of India is at stake.

India should invite multinational companies to improve job prospects. Ground work should be laid by Indian Public or Private sector companies – so that the multinational ventures do not waste time nor lose money in the initial stages of business (reduce transaction cost) start up. These multinational companies should be able to buy part of public or private sector industries. They should be able to start manufacturing in India immediately on plant installation, so that they do not lose millions of dollars.

The incoming companies should have the option of joint ventures or acquiring part of Public Sector Companies without losing money in initial stages of business. The Indian Public sector industry should be ready with flexible organizational structure. They should be ready with land, licenses if required, operational factories with some labor and management.

India At The Crossroads

Micro credit

Micro credit

Mahatma Gandhi has said:

"The soul of India lies in her villages."

The real India lives in her villages. This is as true today as it was 65 years ago when India became independent. Mahatma Gandhi believed in experiments in truth and changing with the times. He would have loved to see the 600 towns in the hubs of rural areas improve as much as the big cities. He would have loved to see jobs or self-employment for all rural people.

Over 70% of India's population lives in villages. The vastness, the variety, the vitality, the color and indeed the very pulse of India, is to be experienced in its villages. Most urbanites view rural India as a peaceful place, where people live a simple and honest life: where the land is green and the air is pure. Though some of these images are accurate depictions, the realities of the day-to-day life and conditions faced by the majority of rural people is pathetic with harsh reality of poverty, neglect and helplessness.

Inescapable debt faced by rural communities

When a man or woman borrows any amount of money, no matter how small, they must pay high

India At The Crossroads

interest rates and face deplorable terms and conditions. Due to illness in the family or other unfortunate circumstances, it will be virtually impossible for them to work their way out of poverty. This is a serious problem, especially in the rural areas and it has been going on for a long time and must be dealt with almost immediately. This problem of inescapable debt faced by the rural community can be tackled with the aid of bank loans, donations and government aid. One solution for unemployment and poverty in countries like India is wholesale microcredit funds in various regions of the country. Indian banks should run microcredit programs where employees are adequately trained, and an effective management system structure is in place. Banks can create a microcredit branch or subsidiary with trained staff.

Fortunately, now there are Indian private banks and foreign banks in India, in addition to nationalized banks. The Government of India should encourage and give incentives to these banks to open and give loans to rural people, especially the poor. One way to encourage banks is to allow part of government business to them, when they open branches in rural areas and give money to rural poor as microloans. At present these government businesses are restricted to nationalized banks only. Encouraging nationalized banks to open more branches in these rural areas and give money as loans to poor people would also be greatly beneficial. Moreover, the banking industry should see this as opportunity and realize that these

Micro credit

microcredit borrowers should be considered as pre-bankable.

Microcredit is very small loan to the unemployed, to poor entrepreneurs and to others living in poverty, who are not considered bankable. Most of these people lack collateral, steady employment and a credit history and therefore cannot even qualify for traditional credit from the banks. Indian businesses continue to grow but not everyone is benefiting from this in the rural areas. In the absence of tiny loans from banks, poor people must borrow money from loan sharks who charge very high interest from those who are desperate for a little cash. Once a man or women borrows any amount, it is impossible for them to get out of a debt trap and many times even have to sell their land and house to pay back the loan.

"The poor stay poor not because they are lazy, but because they have no access to capital."

--Milton Friedman

(1976 Noble Prize winner in Economic Sciences)

In India, the National Bank for Agriculture and Rural Development (NABARD), Rural Development Bank (RDB), Co-operative Banks (CBs) are encouraging commercial banks to lend money to the poor through Self-Help Group (SHG) methodology. NGOs provide support in forming SHGs, training the members to maintain account books and manage their savings.

The amount involved in these programs and other programs, although useful, is negligible; comparable to a drop of water in a bucket. The loans should be increased by at least 100 times in order to have a real impact on the economy.

Microfinance is emerging as an influential and high-potential industry in its own right. C.Rangarajan's committee on financial inclusion submitted its final report on Jan.4, 2008 that microfinance institutions "could play a significant role in facilitating inclusion, as they are uniquely positioned in reaching out to the rural poor." The government has underscored financial inclusion as one way to reduce poverty. With micro credit people can be assisted to rise above poverty, even with an incredibly low amount of money. Cost per person is very low because microcredit loans are paid back and the money is recycled to help yet another poor family. The greatest motivation for borrowers to repay their loans is to qualify for larger, follow-up loans. When an entrepreneur steps out of the revolving loans cycle because his or her business has grown strong enough to stand on its own, he or she has overcome the curse of poverty. Once the small business succeeds, they can get a loan from the bank on the usual terms.

Micro finance companies should have the same benefits as enjoyed by banks so that they would be able to lower their interest rates, reach more

Micro credit

customers and help hundreds of millions more to lift out of poverty. Micro finance companies are now well-regulated, supervised and follow many of the same kind of qualifying requirements as banks. Yet banks enjoy preferential fiscal policies that micro finance companies and their poor clients do not. Microfinance provides financial services from small loans to insurance, to millions of unbanked households. Banks enjoy many beneficial tax reductions and exemptions but microfinance companies do not. Microfinance companies also pay service taxes that their poor customers end up paying even though they should be exempt.

The Government should waive service tax on all micro-loans and micro-insurance products which are under Rs 25,000. The middle and upper classes get tax breaks on insurance premiums and on interest on housing loans. Micro finance companys' customers, most of whom are illiterate and live in remote villages, do not file tax returns and therefore can't benefit from tax refunds. The rural poor still pay a 1% to 2% processing fee on their micro-loans as well as service taxes of about 10% on their micro-insurance policies. Banks can claim deductions of 10% on assets classified as doubtful or loss assets. Financial institutions get a tax deduction of 7.5% of gross total income for reserves kept against possible bad debts.

In India if we mobilize the economy and allocate resources almost immediately and move fast, we can eliminate poverty in the next five years. In villages, each family member under the poverty line could be given from the nationalized banks of India a loan of Rs 10,000 in the first year, going up to Rs 20,000 in the second year, and so on and others could start with Rs 20,000, go up to Rs 40,000 the next year, and so on. This process will continue with higher loan amounts. With typically 98% repayment rate for good microcredit programs, the cost to the government will be nothing because it is only a loan. In the next five years the average income for these villagers will be doubled. In the next ten years no one will be under the poverty line. Conditions will continue to improve for these rural people. Ultimately these loans could be operational with IT help as India will see a huge increase of computers, solar and wind energy in villages.

Nationalized banks and micro financial companies should also hire local people and rely on group lending for repayment. If one member of a joint borrowing group defaults, the others cannot get credit, so they put social pressure on the defaulter and also render moral persuasion to make him to pay up. Also the defaulter can get advice on financial problems. Some borrowers may get into trouble when they cannot pay back their loan. The bank should still feel that it is their responsibility to help them. The banks should make their rules very flexible so that they can adjust to the requirements of the borrower. Banks should also provide cash through emergency loan

Micro credit

programs if needed. Presently these human concerns don't exist for traditional banks. The biggest incentive for the burrowers to pay back their loans should be to build credit for additional loans. To make it more humane, an emergency loan program should be implemented by banks with the cooperation of the local governments, charity from businesses and individuals (in case of droughts, natural disaster, unemployment or illness in the family). Additionally, long term loans should be given in case the family does not have income or lose their income.

Nationalized banks should employ and train local rural people to work in rural areas, who know the culture of the area. The usual argument that banks do not have sufficient qualified staff to go to rural areas is not correct, nor fair to rural poor. Rural poor-households are still left out, while non-poor households have got loans in urban areas. Nationalized banks and microfinance companies have yet to reach large areas in rural India. When Indian banks were nationalized in 1969, workers were not sufficiently qualified, yet the banks survived and flourished. The usual practice is to train new people on the job. The same thing was done in Bangladesh. Also there is need for on the job training in banks, insurance companies, agri-business and microfinance institutions in rural areas with local talent, as was done in China and many other countries.

Microcredit loans by Nationalized Banks

India At The Crossroads

Nationalization of banks was done for the benefit of the poor people of India. Unfortunately, the benefits of nationalized banks have, by and large, not reached the poor. Nationalized banks and micro finance companies should reach people in rural areas. There is political patronage in giving loans by the nationalized banks. Households getting microcredit now outnumber poor households. Outstanding microfinance loans total 80 million. Some borrowers have multiple loans, so net beneficiaries may be a total of 60 million households. This is more than a quarter of India's 220 million households in urban areas.

In addition to microloans to individuals, tiny and small manufacturing units in villages should be encouraged by the government. Labor intensive products like textile, leather, agro-food, automotive spare parts and electrical goods manufactured by small and medium sized industries should be given loans by the banks. The manufacturing sector of solar and wind energy is likely to be the future of India. The country could take major advantage of the newly emerging opportunities and even make up for earlier ones missed. India must act on these opportunities promptly, as microcredit to individuals and other loans to small manufacturing units in these rural areas will be crucial for uplifting the rural masses.

Education and vocational training are most important for farmers to succeed in agricultural practices and in

Micro credit

other fields. If three quarters (75%) of their families can successfully make money in the non-agriculture field, the lives of those living in villages will be changed completely for the better.

India specializes in the advancement of software and we should use this in manufacturing sector in terms of applications. The best application will be in the field of renewable power, especially in solar and wind energy and connecting it with the power grid. With microcredit people in rural areas can own units of solar and wind energy and can sell energy to the power grid. This can be a very profitable small and mini business for millions of people. Software has been labor-intensive in India, for those who are educated in software engineering, creating immense opportunity. Indian agriculture will coexist in villages with manufacturing and services.

As growth occurs, India will reach wonders in the telecommunication industry. Extending the national grid to all remote villages of the country would be a gigantic task and also very expensive. But ultimately that would happen as it did in Western countries. Currently, the best option is wind turbines and solar power -- and connecting them to the national power grid at a later stage. Many other alternative energy solutions are in the pipe line and could be more economical in the future.

There is a shortage of wind turbines and solar power units throughout the world. In the Indian public sector there are many government subsidiaries owned by the centre and states. These and their subsidiaries should manufacture solar panels and wind turbines, and should supply these units to customers on easy payment terms. Customers can pay in easy monthly installments over a period of three to four years with the help of banks. Some people will buy a single solar unit and share it with their neighbors while others will sell the power to national grid. This could become a small or mini business for millions of people in villages. This way a small income is generated for the owner of the unit and the benefit of electricity is spread to many families.

The central government should make needed investments that private enterprises cannot or would not make on its own. They should increase liquidity or direct bank spending, to stimulate demand in rural India. The services sector in rural India should be encouraged by the government. The service sector will not only make money, but will also employ a good proportion of people. This is true particularly for their self-employment, with abilities ranging from simple skills to super skills.

India has not taken full advantage of globalization

Six decades after independence, we still have many major problems to solve. It seems India does not have the type of resolve that is required to wipe out centuries of stagnation and poverty and emerge as a vibrant society. India has completely ignored the rural areas and its people. India has let go of many opportunities presented by technology, as well as trade and business. People in the rural areas have been starved of microcredit. China (first through Hong Kong and then directly) and many other Asian countries have taken considerable advantage of Globalization over the last forty years. Meanwhile, India could not take advantage of Globalization to the same extent. The biggest problem is that the central government and state governments have so much deficit and debt and are very much limited to the improvements they can achieve.

In Indian clusters of villages, in new towns or in mini-new cities, the service sector will be a major part of the economy. Trading, including marketing and goods for sale: shoes, medicine, furniture, clothing, jewelry, DVDs, foodstuff, repairing will be increased considerably. Additionally, various forms of government services, the postal services, teaching, banking, financial services, real estate, human resources, media and advertising, will be propelled by changes in agriculture and manufacturing in rural areas. Improvement in many of the fields mentioned above will open up many new opportunities for those who are self-employed. Microcredit will greatly benefit these self-employed people to make their work as productive as possible.

With new technology - new windows of opportunities

The rate at which technology offers new solutions and new windows of opportunity is fortunately very high in the current phase of human development, especially in the field of renewable energy. Indians can make up for the lost time and missed opportunities, provided they learn to move fast. The opportunities left will not be around long as China and other countries have already grabbed many of them. Capital to rural India must be provided on a large scale for development to take place. Small loans to individuals for their small businesses are also necessary so that their families do not starve.

Microcredit biggest job provider

In India, demand is high for savings services of the banks. Poor people need some bank which will hold and protect the little bit of cash a villager can gather; an extra animal they have raised, or money they have hidden in their shanty. These small amounts are not considered by banks good enough (or large enough) to save in the bank. So they hide their small savings at places which are not secure. Earning interest on savings deposits is unheard of and a dream for most of them. In India about 70% of rural poor do not have a deposit account, 87% have no access to credit from banks, 85% of households do not have any kind of insurance and a very few (less than 0.4%) have access to health insurance and 600 micro finance institutions have a cumulative outreach of 12.5 million poor households, representing only 5% of people in the country. Banks, micro finance institutions, development financial institutions and civil society organizations should all be encouraged by the governments to give loans to all rural people in India. It will be the biggest job provider sector in India.

Economists believe that the only way to create jobs for hundreds of millions of people is the government and private capital investment in big projects. The only employment that most economics textbooks recognize is wage employment. They overlook the small businesses owned by individuals who earn their living this way so that their family does not starve. Indian poverty can be eliminated because India has the technology and resources to do so. All that is needed is the will to succeed and then putting the necessary institutions and policies in place for it to happen. The rich, middle class and most urbanites tend to be so busy with their everyday work and enjoyment with little thought or regard for the starving and poor rural people.

Microcredit catalyst for self-employment

Economists have missed out on an essential feature of economic reality. Economic principles do not have a place for people making a living through self-employment. But in the real world, especially in rural

India, that is what the poor are doing, creating income through self-employment. Microcredit for the poor can create self-employment and generate income. There is nothing wrong with the government creating jobs and encouraging other industries to create jobs. But people do not have to wait generations for that to happen. In India, for generations, people are involved in small businesses or self-employment. People are still very poor and starving because they never received loans from banks or other sources at a reasonable rate of interest.

In rural India most people are surviving with self-employment in different fields. Everywhere in India agriculture is the mainstay of the people. Many vegetable growers grow vegetables for sale to wholesale agents or act as sales agents themselves. A large number of them take up the sale of cash crop and their by-products as a source of livelihood. Chilies, vegetables such as brinjal, ladysfinger, different kinds of gourds, mushroom, beans, ginger, onions, potatoes, bananas and other types of fruits, cashew and jackfruit, coconut and coir, flowers and other agriculture products. Hundreds of women members trained in tailoring, do job work for agents who supply the thriving readymade textile market. The products they make range from towels, handkerchiefs and petticoats to shirts and trousers. This tailoring job or business can be multiplied with bank loans, micro finance and with a little bit of training on sewing machines.

Micro credit

The assumption that self-employment is merely a temporary stop-gap occupation is wrong. Self-employment is not a new thing for India. Self-employment has been practiced from time memorial and it will continue because of the type of India's economy and its population. There are hardly 10% of people in the organized sector with job security. Self-employment is giving livelihood to hundreds of millions of Indians and it will stay and prosper. People should have options to choose from, including jobs and self-employment. A very large number of people in India do both, a menial job and a small business like milking cows, some handicrafts work, weaving etc. When provided with a microloan, they can choose what they want to do.

Some self-employed men and women are engaged in handicrafts like making of grass mats, terracotta clay pots, baskets and mats, stone sculptures and bronze figurines are all made at home. Handicrafts are often indigenous to the region. The crafts display the extraordinary skill that comes from generations of close observation and practice. Others are engaged in the craft of weaving floor mats and carpets. Some are engaged in making cushion covers, table mats, CD holders, handbags and fans. Special 'signature' wedding paais woven with the names of bridal couples are particularly popular. The finer weaves like the soft pattu paai ('silk paai') are more expensive as they require skills of a higher order and take more time. Many embroiders are engaged in embroidery work on saris. Some traditional crafts groups do both design-to-order and supply to any place in India as well as to the export market. These people are very innovative and if given proper training on how to use sewing machines and other stitching machines, they (India) can export as much as China is exporting.

In the book *'Creating a World Without poverty'*, Muhammad Yunus writes:

> Economists are wedded to this approach (wage employment) to alleviating poverty because the only kind of employment that most economics textbooks recognize is wage employment. The textbook world is made up solely of "firms" and "farms" that hire different qualities of labor at different wage levels. There is no room in economic literature for making a living through self-employment, finding ways to develop goods or services that they sell directly to those who need them. But in the real world, that is what you see the poor doing everywhere (page 53).

There are many small industries which are run by one family or small group of people as self-employed: papad making, masala (spices) making, bakery, popcorn, paddy (rice) processing, dal/pulses, processing of edible and non-edible oil seeds, footwear, leather goods, tannery, bone crushing, leather, flaying, match, rolling agarbetthis (incense sticks), fireworks, gur, khandsari, palm candy,

Micro credit

palmfibre brush, palm leaf mats, tappers, toilet soap, laundry soap, non-edible oil processing, handmade paper, pottery, brick bhatta unit, porcelain chinaware, stone wear unit, brick clamp, two ply yarn making (sisal).

Grass mat, table mat, sisal fiber production, carpenter home unit (hand tools), blacksmith home unit (hand tools), lime shell burning, lime production, quarrying, marble stone art ware unit, katha manufacturing, readymade garments, handloom, hosiery, toys and doll making, embroidery, surgical bandages, batik work, fruit processing and preservation, handmade utensils, electronic clocks, candle and sealing wax, shampoos, detergents and washing powder, hair oils, manufacture of rubber goods (dipper latex products), umbrella assembly, hand carts, bullock carts, small boats, paper safety & stone pins, sweet & snacks and so on.

In Bangladesh, 85% of poor families have already been reached by microcredit. The projection is that nearly 100% of poor families in Bangladesh will be reached by 2012, making it the first country in the world to bring financial services to every poor family. In Bangladesh poor people are trained in social activities collectively to create a new generation to take families out of reach of poverty. (Grameen Bank was started by Muhammad Yunus, winner of the Nobel Peace Prize, to give small and tiny loans to poor people of Bangladesh.) In addition to Grameen

Bank principles of discipline, unity, courage and hard work, the borrowers are encouraged to educate their children. Those that have been reached by microcredit come from varying financial and familial circumstances but they all share in the happiness, success and fulfillment that have been brought to their lives as a result of microcredit.

Grameen Bank of Bangladesh encourages persons to start businesses on their own

At Grameen Bank unemployed persons are encouraged to start businesses of their own. When a borrower does not want to borrow money, saying that they have no business experience, the loan officer will encourage and try to convince them that they can come up with an idea for a business of their own, even if it is their first experience. A very large number of people start their small businesses and succeed and thus benefit with microcredit this way. Some borrowers get into trouble and cannot even pay back their loan and still the banks feel that it is their responsibility to help them. They make their rules very flexible so that they can adjust to the requirements of the borrower.

Indian rural people may be poor and most do not have a formal education, but they are talented, inventive, hardworking and highly entrepreneurial. Microcredit investment is needed for these people so that they can advance themselves and the

Micro credit

generations that follow. What the average person would consider pocket change can represent a doubling of income for impoverished people. The result of microcredit programs that provide loans to poor can be seen and felt easily as their financial condition improves. As poor families cease being poor, prosperity and happiness is visible. Their vicious circle breaks and microcredit reverses their lives to an upward trend.

Most of Indian rural poor people live in a cash only economy. They have no facilities for bank loans or other financial services. They would find it difficult to expand sales for their tiny businesses, as their inventory of clothes or garments, produce or basic household items would be limited to what their meager profit would buy. Since they have no reserves, small emergencies would turn into disaster and their small business capital would be completely wiped out.

Income derived from microcredit is not large, neither is the cost of living of the individuals who use or run them. That is why the minor increase in income, which is generated from appropriate use of microcredit, can give families the financial help necessary to increase their standard of living. With loans, businesses can grow and move their families even further up the economic ladder. This is real progress, perhaps the first progress, some families have seen in generations. Working with passion, parents are ensuring that their children will not suffer as they have. Most rural Indians are intelligent and hard-working. They know that if they do not work, their families do not eat.

Microcredit adds no cost to governments -- as loans are re-paid

The encouraging result of several organizations is that repayment rates for good microcredit programs exceed 98%, primarily because of cross-guarantees and the incentive of additional loans. When it is required, microcredit collections are just as effective as traditional collection agencies, only more personal and creative. The debt collection task falls to a loan officer. The loan officer is usually a local who grew up in the community; he understands the culture and knows what he needs to do. In the absence of microcredit, poor people who resort to borrowing money are likely to do so by borrowing from loan sharks who will charge very high interest from those who are desperate for a little cash. The loan sharks will then force them to sell their land at throw away prices. Interest on microloans is much lower and reasonable.

Commercial Banks and other conventional financial institutions seldom lend to low-income families and women-headed households. Commercial lending institutions require that borrowers have a stable source of income out of which principal and interest can be paid back every month. The income of many self-employed rural households is not stable. A large number of small loans are needed to serve the poor, but lenders prefer dealing with large loans in small numbers to minimize administration costs. They consider low income households a bad risk and look for collateral with a clear title, which many low-income households do not have.

Microcredit -- a most effective poverty relieving strategy

Poor people when given access to timely financial services at market rates, repay their loans and use the proceeds to increase their income and assets. This is not surprising since the only realistic alternative for them is to borrow at an interest much higher than market rates. Community banks, NGOs and grass root savings and credit groups around the world have shown that these microloans can be profitable both for borrowers and lenders, making microfinance one of the most effective poverty reducing strategies.

Some of the important benefits of microcredit exceed merely financial benefits -- and cannot be measured on a balance sheet. The true benefits are dignity and self-esteem, along with respect for family and education for the children. In the absence of any financial help or microcredit, some poor people and their children become beggars and many children work as slave labor. Microcredit should not be seen as charity but rather as the opportunity poor people need to build a decent life.

More than half of India's population of 1.3 billion would most certainly benefit from microcredit. Microcredit is capital-starved because few people know about it and understand how and why it works. By providing some capital, you can help poor people advance their small businesses with small loans. With loans they can achieve stability and the dignity that comes from solving their own problems. Banks should also provide cash through emergency loan programs. Presently these human concerns don't exist for traditional banks.

The rural poor of today will be consumers and entrepreneurs of tomorrow. The following is a quote from Dr. C.K.Prahalad, Management expert at the University of Michigan, USA and author of several books:

> If we stop thinking of the poor as victims or as a burden and start recognizing them as resilient and creative entrepreneurs and value conscious consumers, a whole new world of opportunity will open up.

For lenders and NGOs other types of financial leverage may also be possible, including letter of credit, grants to microcredit projects from governmental organizations, bank loans, donations,

Micro credit

borrowed money and through religious organizations. In India some people give money to charitable organizations and of course claim benefits from income tax. The real test of their charity work should be to see how it is benefiting the poor. These rich donors should spend a little bit of their own time to see that their charity is going to the right people. These decisions on charities should be made judiciously. The CEO or the chief executive of the donors company should appoint a dedicated person for this cause. A donor who gives money to different organizations should know how many lives he or she has improved and in what way.

In India there are thousands of religious teachers and members of faith who are preaching self-improvement and how to attain peace of mind. Their teachings are beneficial for the self-improvement of the disciples or the devotees as well as benefit the religious teachers financially. Shouldn't half of a preacher's time be spent guiding their disciples to spend time and money improving the economic conditions of the less fortunate? After all, this is the biggest service to God. This should be done for at least the next five to ten years until there are no poor people, no homeless people and no beggars.

In India services offered by Gurdwaras and churches should be the model for all the people to follow. All the rich and middle class people should give to poor institutions as it is done in the USA, Canada and

Europe. Their aim should be that there remain no poor and starving people in India.

The advice (for especially the rich) given by President John F. Kennedy in the United States in his inaugural address on January 20th, 1961 was:

> "And so, my fellow Americans, ask not what your country can do for you – Ask what you can do for your country."

In the book *'A Billion Bootstrap'* by Phil Smith & Eric Thurman, it is written:

> When a micro business succeeds or strengthened, the entrepreneur and his or her family reap the benefits of immediate, usually sustained and often permanent, income increase. The children grow up healthier and better educated. The family's subsequent generations may be spared the poverty which this generation was born into. The entrepreneur who is making more money in turn spends more money on local goods and services, which upgrades the local economy and creates more jobs. This ripple effect becomes exponential through the generations. As children grow up more prosperous than the previous generation, they purchase more goods and services (page 70) [...] My rule of thumb is that it takes a net cost of about 1% of the average annual per capita income of a

Micro credit

country to move one person up the economic ladder using microcredit (page 73).

A donor who gives money to different organizations, wants to know how many lives he or she has improved and in what way. To calculate the cost to improve economic conditions per person Phil Smith, estimated how many times donations will circulate by a recycled loan. If the money is circulated a minimum of 20 times (twenty years of one-year loans), every $1,000 contributed eventually will provide at least $20,000 in microloans. As in case of rural India, it is reasonable to expect that families have five members. Multiply the loan recycle rate 20 (twenty years of one-year loans) by the number of family members (5) means that every donation directly changes the lives of 100 people (children and adults). 100 becomes part of the formula in the final steps of the calculations. The last step is to divide the country's average annual per capita income by 100 to calculate the cost per person. This calculation yields an answer that is exactly 1% of a country's average annual per capita income.

According to the World Bank, in 2005 the average annual per capita income for India was $720. India's cost to improve economic condition per person is $7.20 according to Phil Smith. Clearly these numbers are approximate, but to help people bring themselves out of deadly poverty for a cost of $7.20 per person sounds ridiculously low. These figures are approximate and may seem too good to be true, but they are realistic. Cost per person becomes amazingly low with microcredit because loans are paid back and the money is recycled to help yet another family of poor people. It could take a decade before your return on investment reaches its full potential. Results however will show within three years. This is why supporting micro-credit is so appealing to donors with business acumen. When you calculate, it is hard to imagine any other humanitarian service that can produce such impressive results.

In the past, the next generation had no reason to expect they could exceed the financial status of their parents. Today most of the children whose families have benefited from microcredit *loans* are receiving elementary education, which is certainly a middle-class achievement by any standards. This success is changing lives.

In *'The World is Flat'* by Thomas L. Friedman, he observes that when people have hope, they are a part of the middle class:

> They have a pathway out of poverty or lower-income status towards a higher standard of living and a better future for their kids. You can be middle class in your head whether you make $2 a day or $200, if you believe in social mobility -- that your kids have a chance to live better than you do -- and that hard work and playing by the rules of your society will get you

Micro credit

where you want to go.

Summary

The conditions and realities of the day-to-day life faced by the majority of rural people are pathetic with harsh reality of poverty, neglect and helplessness.

Indian businesses continue to grow but not everyone is benefiting from this in the rural areas. In the absence of tiny loans from banks, poor people must borrow money from loan sharks who charge very high interest from those who are desperate for a little cash.

Fortunately now there are Indian private banks and foreign banks in India in addition to nationalized banks. The Government of India should encourage and give incentives to these banks to open and give loans to rural people, especially to the poor.

Microcredit will substantially increase the banks' business. Also the financial position of the people will improve considerably with microloans in terms of personal life and business.

Microcredit for the poor can create self-employment and generate income. In India, for generations people have been involved in small businesses or self-employment. In rural India most people are surviving with self-employment in different fields. Most of the poor rural people live in a cash only economy.

Through providing some capital, governments can help poor people advance their small businesses with small loans.

Nationalized banks and microfinance companies have yet to reach large areas in rural India. Nationalization of banks was done for the benefit of the poor people of India. Nationalized banks and micro finance companies should reach people in rural areas. India has completely ignored the rural areas and its people. People in the rural areas have been starved of microcredit.

Nationalized banks, micro finance Institutions, development financial institutions, civil society organizations, non-governmental organizations should increase their funds considerably to reach people in rural areas. India has completely ignored the rural areas and therefore those people have been starved of microcredit. This is because they were never introduced to microcredit. Banks should also provide cash through emergency loan program. Presently these human concerns don't exist for traditional banks.

Some borrowers may get into trouble and cannot pay back their loan. The bank should still feel that it is their responsibility to help them. The banks should make their rules very flexible so that they can adjust to the requirements of the borrower.

Micro credit

For generations, the people of India have been involved in small businesses or self-employment. In rural India most people are surviving with self-employment in different fields. Most of India's rural poor people live in a cash only economy. They have no facilities for bank loans or other financial services. By providing some capital, you can help poor people advance their small businesses with small loans.

India At The Crossroads

Education in Rural India

India At The Crossroads

Education in Rural India

The government is committed to ensuring universal Elementary education at the Primary and Upper Primary level for all children 6-14 years of age. In India, the main types of schools are those controlled by the state government boards, in which the vast majority of Indian school children are enrolled. India now has a new Right to Education Act. The government has finalized the sharing of funds in the ratio of 65 to 35 between the centre and the states for implementing the law making education a fundamental right. The Right of Children to Free and Compulsory Education Act provides free and compulsory education for every child between the ages of 6-14.

Pre-Primary education in India on the other hand is not a fundamental right, thus there is a very low percentage of children attending the Preschool educational facilities in the rural areas. Children should begin attending school at the age of 4. Unfortunately many children in India do not receive education until the age of 6 starting in Grade one, while others start private school at the age of 4 in lower Kindergarten.

Children in rural areas, especially those from poor families are at a disadvantage. Children who start school at the late age of 6 are missing out 2 years of education. These early years of education are essential to a child's growth and development. A child who starts school at 6 will likely have difficulties learning to read, whereas their peers who have been educated from a very young age are far more likely to make a smooth transition into learning to read and write effectively.

In the absence of significant government provisions, private sector (reaching to the relatively richer section of society) has opened schools. Provisions in these kindergartens are divided into two stages – lower Kindergarten (LKG) and upper Kindergarten (UKG). Typically, a LKG class is comprised of children 3 to 4 years of age, and the UKG class is comprised of children 4 to 5 years of age. After finishing upper Kindergarten, a child enters Grade 1of Primary school.

English classes should begin from Grade 1

The English language should be taught beginning at the Grade 1 level. Presently, English classes start in many states from Grade 1 and in other states from higher grades, especially in rural India. Most children in rural India struggle with the rules of grammar and in turn they come to despise the English language altogether. The trick is to have students learn the spoken language first, then grammar. Teaching-aids such as TVs, CDs and DVDs should be provided to assist with learning English in Indian schools. Some international English tapes should be provided to students in school libraries so that proper pronunciation and accent can be picked up from early childhood.

The Chinese government moved in 2001 to mandate English language training in Grade 3, instead of Grade 7, which had been the practice. Canada's Lingo Media made an agreement with the People's Education Publisher almost a decade ago to help create English-as-a-Foreign Language books for China's early Primary grades. An author team comprised some of the best known creators of children's educational materials in Canada. The team developed new materials for the Chinese market. This team visited schools, teachers and their Chinese counter parts in publishing.

The end result of the Chinese-Canadian collaboration is a colorfully illustrated series of books that relies heavily on music, poetry, rhythm and other tricks to help Chinese children learn to speak English, not just read it. In Lingo Media's case the chief export is intellectual capital and managerial talent. The actual books are printed and published in China to keep the cost down. It has sold, with its joint venture partner, some 30 million copies of its books in the first few years (about 6 years ago). These language books are sold and used in Primary classrooms across China. The English language has become a national fascination in China. These books helped Chinese children immensely to read, write and speak better English. These low cost printed and published books and other books for children have developed a very big export market for China.

Chinese's demography, a one-child policy has created a nation of pampered youngsters and expectation has grown from these children. Parents and grandparents are putting emphasis on education as never before. The whole family's future rests on that one child's success, which in turn translates into a national obsession with education. In India the population is multiplying. By 2025 India's population will be 1.5 billion while China will be at one billion. In the near future China won't have any uneducated or poor people, while it is likely that India will remain with half the population uneducated and poor, especially in rural areas.

Difficult Hindi words and grammar should be avoided

Spoken simple Hindi is understood in most part of India. Hindi movies and songs are also very popular throughout India. The problem lies with difficult Hindi words and grammar. Hindi and other regional languages should be kept very simple in the school systems, as with globalization English is needed for employment in India and throughout the world. Too much grammar and difficult words should be avoided in school systems. These languages should be very simple and mostly spoken language should be taught in lower grades only. These languages should not be compulsory in college education.

Learning grammar and vocabulary (very difficult words in Hindi and other regional languages) have spoiled the lives of many students. Because of this compulsion, many students who are knowledgeable in other subjects dropout of schools or colleges. More and more grammar is taught and the rules became an end in themselves. The guardians of the Hindi language became increasingly preoccupied with vocabulary and grammar. Hindi is now understood by all Indians below the age of forty. The spread of Hindi has been due to cinema, television and popular music. Just as English is the language of business and higher education, Hindi is the language of popular culture.

Poor infrastructure of schools result in high dropout rates

The poor infrastructure of schools in rural areas of India has resulted in fairly high dropout rates. Some schools remain single classroom schools often with a single teacher and lack of other facilities. Some schools have leaky roofs and others have broken windows and doors. The average teacher to pupil ratio for the country is 1:36, 8.39% schools are single teacher schools; 5.30% schools have more than 100 children for each teacher; 30.87% schools lack female teachers and do not have washroom facilities for girl students. Only 10.73% schools have a computer. It is no wonder that an NGO report has estimated that out of every 100 village girls enrolling in Class I, only one will survive the system to reach Class XII.

The strategies adopted by the governments to check dropout rates is generating parental awareness, economic incentives and National Program of Nutritional support to Primary Education (Mid-day Meal Scheme) and many other programs. Economic reasons are the most prominent for high dropout rates (see below for current statistics). Poor families need an extra income to earn through their child, however the child could earn very little or hardly any money.

Money grants for weaker children of poor families

The government should give financial help in the form of a scholarship or stipend to children of poor families to enable them to study. This could mean say $10 a month per child.

Economic incentives like jobs for parents and other small financial incentives will be of immense help to reduce the dropout rate. Some sort of voucher or money grants for weaker children of poor families should be given by the government. This could be in the form of private tuition for a small group of students by a senior student. The payment for this could be made by something like guaranteed employment for the rural who are educated. This will help in reducing the dropout rates in government schools in rural areas. Almost all mothers of students in rural areas are uneducated. Whereas in urban areas, educated mothers help their children with their home work. With this extra support and guidance, these students will perform significantly better in school and the dropout rate will decreased considerably.

High stress levels, low recognition and low salary for their talents put teachers in the position of having to leave their vocation. Teacher training has remained moribund, and commercialization is the only change taking place. China offers free teacher training for aspiring teachers and it would be wise for India to do the same. Teachers have a trade union which protects them whether they teach or not. Therefore many rural teachers do not even come to school at all. In light of this, the number of teachers should be increased considerably. The payment could be made by something along the lines of guaranteed employment for the educated people. Teacher helpers should be provided for schools so that when teachers are absent, teaching and knowledge will still be imparted to the students. Teaching aids should also be provided such as TVs, CDs and DVDs specially designed for student learning.

More teachers needed in schools

Teachers unions in schools, are like central government, state governments, municipalities, public undertakings, and nationalized Bank unions. The difference is that in central government, state governments, municipalities, public undertakings, and nationalized banks, the number of employees are about two to four times more than required. If the same standard was applied to teachers, the number of teachers required or needed would be greatly increased. The government's most damaging failure is in the public education sector. Many studies have shown that one out of four teachers are absent at any given time. One out of two present is not teaching at any given time. What is also noteworthy is the large dropout rate at the primary education level. Fifty percent of students leave school before fifth grade.

Socio-economic conditions are the major cause of education deprivation among children. The poor make one dollar a day. The National sample survey organization states that twenty percent of people in rural areas earn only Rs. 12 a day. Any medical crisis pushes them towards loan sharks. In the absence of bank loans or microcredit from other sources, sometimes these people resort to selling their land.

Government school education has become so bad that even poor Indians have begun pulling their children out of government schools, enrolling them in private schools which charge $1 to $3 a month in fees. Private schools have become prominent, spreading rapidly in slums and villages across India. Private schools in India range from expensive boarding schools for the elite to low-end teaching shops in markets. Although teacher's salaries are on average considerably lower in private schools, their students perform much better. A recent national study led by Pratham, an Indian nongovernmental

Education in Rural India

organization, found that even in small villages, 16 percent of children are attending private Primary schools. These students scored 10 per cent higher on verbal and mathematics exams than those in public schools.

A New York Times article dated Aug 16, 2007 brought to our attention, "after 60 years of independence, nearly 30 percent of Indians still live below the official poverty line and close to half of all Indian children under the age of three are malnourished". The Economist quotes the National Commission for Enterprises in the Un-organized sector saying, 836 million Indians "live on less than 20 rupees a day, the equivalent of about 50 cents American. Even high growth and smart macroeconomic reforms are not enough in a democracy. Prime Minister, Manmohan Singh is aware that India's economic success has not been equally shared. Cities have done better than villages and some states have done better than others.

Every educational project in rural India must be given funds to be completed in double-quick time. Governments should ensure that projects are started and completed on schedule. Many projects are still born on the drawing boards because we have peculiar notions of cost/benefit ratio. These sophisticated calculations do not take into account the enormous benefits that will flow from educating and employing millions of men and women reaching money to their households in the form of wages, rather than through dubious subsidies and doles.

Software and business-process outsourcing exports have grown from practically nothing to $35 billion. The constraining factor is likely not demand but the ability of India's educational system to produce enough quality English-speaking (engineering) graduates. With some help from the government, many rural students can be educated to take up these jobs.

School curriculum should be Interesting and relevant

In the context of curriculum, few are bothered about the burden of dullness and irrelevance certain content impose on children. Children have no opportunity for practical hands-on experience which is essential for learning. Something as basic as a geometry box seems a luxury for a student studying in a village school. Enthusiasm and imagination are conspicuously lacking in the educational system that is provided for these village children. The most basic and fundamental teaching aids such as maps, chalk, and globes are not available in primary schools. Teachers in rural areas are not trained to run activity-centered classrooms, nor are they provided the necessary materials and resources to do so.

Many argue that India cannot afford an enriched school environment in its vast network of rural schools. Education becomes a joyless burden in our

Education in Rural India

schools because the quality of India's curricula, texts, teaching and examining procedures are so poor. One must ask why India can meet global standards in civil aviation, software and defense and not in its provision for educating rural children. To cope with the educational challenges in rural India, countless government, NGO and private bodies have already researched and discussed in policy paper virtually all the things that need to be changed. A huge investment into primary and secondary education is required.

NREGA should be given to teacher's helper and TVs, DVDs, CDs could be used in school libraries

In the future, education will be massively dependent on the use of IT to reduce cost and improve quality. A cost effective educational programming should be presented on television and radios 24 hours a day on one or more channels. Such programs are already available in India, however much more can be created and obtained from foreign sources. In addition to classroom studies, these TV programs, DVDs and CDs could be used in the school libraries.

If students require help, a teacher helper may be provided to the students. Something similar to the National Rural Employment Guarantee scheme for rural educated, may pay the teacher helpers. To start with, teacher helpers need not be fully trained teachers; many fresh, well-educated Grade 10 graduates, with a little training can be teacher helpers. There are many unemployed Grade 10 graduates available in rural areas.

When the regular teacher is absent or when extra help in the classroom is required, a teacher helper should be able to work as a coordinator. He or she does not have to be highly qualified. Teacher helpers should be from the same village so that they can join duty when needed. They should be trained to operate TV and CDs. In the absence of teachers, or in addition to them, the teacher assistant can engage students in many activities and offer one-on-one support to struggling students. In some countries these types of teachers are called supply teachers, they are called to teach when needed to replace the teacher who is absent.

The majority of school dropout children belong to poor families. The disadvantage of being poor is more felt in the higher age group, with exceedingly high dropout rates within the age group of 11-14, in low-income families.

The Indian Constitution mandates universal education for all. Yet, 50% of children do not reach Grade 5 in India. More than sixty five years after India's political independence, India is placed 126th out of 175 countries ranked in the 2006 Human Development report. 50% of today's Indian adults cannot even read and write a short story, or simple statements relating to their everyday life, or write a simple letter in Hindi,

Education in Rural India

regional languages, or English. Moreover, they cannot even do simple arithmetic. They are cheated by unscrupulous people throughout their lives. India's meager adult literacy rate of 50% can be compared to that of China's exemplary rate of 90%.

The most devastating impact on India's educational system is that they are condemning themselves to a future of exceedingly low employment and economic development, especially in rural India. Even very smart tiny businesses cannot grow because workers have been cheated out of a proper education and have not developed some of the essential skills necessary to excel in their trade. Education is the most important factor in economic growth. Education has a great impact over economic growth, foreign investment and exports.

Around 1948, India had about 250 million illiterate people. Suppose India had taken the big bang approach instead of spending $1 billion that year, it had allocated and spent $10 billion each year for 3 years till 1951 towards Primary education. India would have raised its literacy rate considerably. This cost to the public could have solved the problem once for all. On top of that, having a literate population from 1951 onwards, the aggregate wealth of the country would have been much higher.

NREGA should be provided to school children's parents

The National Rural Employment Guarantee Act (NREGA) should be provided to the parents of school children, where required. The idea is to provide employment to poor and marginal farmers and farm workers. The result will be a reduced dropout rate of rural children once there is some kind of stability for parents by way of an employment guarantee scheme.

China has been much more successful than India in educating and providing jobs to its people. China has managed to increase its employment rapidly, mainly in the manufacturing and construction industry. A cursory look at China shows that poverty declined dramatically in China in the first decade, after economic reforms, because the expanding township and village enterprises absorbed surplus labor in rural areas.

In India this process has not taken roots and there is a vast population of unemployed youth in rural areas which must be gainfully employed. This can be done by using schemes like the employment guarantee scheme to help push the agriculture sector forward. In addition to this, self-employment should be encouraged with micro loans by the banks. Once parents of school children have some financial security, the dropout rate for Primary and Secondary school children would be eliminated completely.

Vocational training classes ought to be offered once a week

Vocational training classes in the school system should be offered once a week, starting from Grade 4. Rural people are mostly doing manual work. They do farming in the fields and some of them need repairs work done on their machinery. Knowledge of operating lathe machines, tractor, truck or car repair will be of immense help to these farmers. Also, some students may develop interest in these fields. They might start their own business in these fields or become mechanics. The reason for starting classes once a week from Grade 4 is that many students may dropout after Grade 5 or Grade 8. With some vocational training experience behind them, these dropouts can build on their acquired practical skills working on a job in that field.

There should be a special class for students who are given a special education in the 3Rs; arithmetic, reading and writing simple, Hindi (regional languages), English. Other subjects like General Knowledge including History and Geography can be taught with the aid of TV, CDs and DVDs in school libraries.

There should be a 'last chance' procedure in place for students planning on dropping out from Grade 5 or Grade 8. This could be implemented in the school system itself. Dropout students should be encouraged and persuaded to continue their education, as well as receive more vocational training. After partition of India in August 1947, many students dropped out and could not continue their education. Punjab University made it very easy for students to appear in their matriculation examinations as a private student throughout India, mostly in Punjab and Delhi.

Thousands of new private schools (low-end teaching shops in markets which were not very expensive) opened up. Many students took private tuition in these schools according to their requirements. After completing their matriculation, these students joined Punjab University or other Universities of India. Millions of people coming out of these universities have done very well in their lives. Similar types of programs should be used for dropout students at Primary and Secondary level in most parts of India by different schools and Universities. Also at that time, many new vocational schools had been started for students who wanted to go into different vocational fields. After completing the vocational schools training, many started their own business and many more got good jobs.

Dropout rates of school children are directly proportionate to the poverty most of the states. UP, Assam, Bihar, Madhya Pradesh and Orissa have a lower level of education. In UP, fifty-three million people, amounting to 31.15 per cent of the population of the state are below the poverty line. Uttar Pradesh accounts for nearly one-eighth of India's population. Each year one million children are growing up illiterate. They will, throughout their lives, remain poor and unemployable; at the most they would get low-grade jobs. The State, because of its misgovernance, is condemning millions of citizens every year to a life of poverty and hopelessness.

Electricity availability has direct impact on education

Electricity can have a dramatic impact on education and literacy. With electricity, children can study at night after they have completed their chores. If India is to have any hope of lifting the yoke of absolute poverty, it must provide rural villages with greater access to electricity. The rich world should help developing countries use clean energy. Unless rich countries help poor countries to leapfrog over the dirtiest energy phases that the rich world went through, the future for all may be needlessly grim. Many drop-out students could study at night to catch up with their studies. India could offer night schools and other TV programs to study at home, even up to the age of 25-30. Some of the programs can be a combination of both night school and other aids like TV and CDs.

Gross Dropout Rate - Classes 1 to 5

Male	39.7%
Female	41.9%

Source: Selected Educational statistics 2000-01, Ministry of Human Resource Development, Government of India (Census of India).

This only includes people who joined the school system.

Summary

In India, the main types of schools are those controlled by the State Government Boards, in which the vast majority of Indian school children are enrolled. India now has a new Right to Education Act. The Right of Children to Free and Compulsory Education Act provides free and compulsory education for every child between the ages of 6-14.

Children should begin attending school at the age of 4. Unfortunately many children in India do not receive education until the age of 6 starting in Grade one, while others start private school at the age of 4 in lower Kindergarten.

The poor infrastructure of schools in rural areas of India has resulted in fairly high dropout rates. Some schools remain single classroom schools and lack other facilities. Many schools in rural areas lack female teachers and do not have washroom facilities for female teachers and students. Fifty percent of students leave school before fifth grade.

Education in Rural India

The majority of school dropout children belong to poor families. Once parents of school children have some financial security, the dropout rate for Primary and Secondary school children would be eliminated completely.

The National Rural Employment Guarantee Act (NREGA) should be provided to parents of school children, where required.

Many times school teachers do not even show up for work. Rural India needs more teachers or teachers' helper. The number of teachers should be increased considerably for students to receive an adequate quality of education. The teacher helper could be paid by the National Rural Employment Guarantee Act (NREGA).

Economic reasons are number one cause for high dropout rates. The government should give financial help in the form of scholarships or stipend to children of poor families. This could be in the form of private tuition by senior students. The payment for this could be made by the governments with something like the National Rural Employment Guarantee Act (NREGA) for rural education.

Vocational Training

India At The Crossroads

Vocational Training

India's population needs basic educational facilities; at least 50% of students should be involved in vocational training after High School. General vocational training classes should be started in schools as a part of the curriculum, because a large number of students will dropout at the Primary level. Once a week, classes should be devoted to vocational training. Indian vocational training for drop out students should be for short duration of a few months (three to six months). Let India b uild this system from ground up on a very large scale. As the drop-out rate decreases and more students in rural areas graduate from High School, the duration and standard can be upgraded. To start with, the technical and vocational education, and training programs should be market-oriented, short-term, and relevant, especially for the rural poor who may be unable to graduate from Grade 8.

Vocational training after grade 8 – or through High School

Instead of increasing the number of colleges for general studies, India should introduce more vocational centres and institutes for the large masses of youth coming out of school. With this in place, by the time the children leave school, they would have developed a skill set, joined an institute and secured a job in that skill, or else started their own small businesses. Even at the school level, it is more appropriate if students are taught useful skills, as a part of the school syllabus. This can be taught as an extra - curricular activity, which students are interested in and enjoy, while also being groomed for that technical skill.

In India the struggle for College and University education is a disaster for all concerned. It seems, India is preparing the youth to become babus (clerks). Existing higher educational facilities are being stretched to a breaking point. The teaching faculty and infrastructure are not able to cope with the increasing number of students.

Vocational education in India is minimal, compared to other countries of the world. India does not spend a sufficient amount of money training its technical students to make India a manufacturing hub. The vocational education percentage in India is at a meager 5% of its total employed workforce of 500 million, as against 95% of South Korea, 80% of Japan and 70% of Germany. This makes a strong case for India to allocate a substantial percentage of its budgetary allocations to promote vocational education to make India a manufacturing hub. Vocational education and training hardly exists in India, especially when compared to China. China has over 500,000 vocational schools, while India has less than 3000 such institutions. Higher and technical education is utterly controlled from the Centre in India. As a

Vocational Training

result there is a shortage of seats and opportunities for higher education.

About 99% of all entrance examination particiipants in the IITs and IIMs are rejected due to capacity constraints. As a result of controlled higher education, the human development index is very low in India leading to multiple problems such as corruption, poverty, unemployment and productivity. The chances of rural students receiving admission into these institutions are almost nill. Rural courses should be practical and the duration should be short, and made simpler to suit the needs of the present condition of rural masses.

India requires vocational training programs to prepare the youth for a vocation of their choice. India should build up a large workforce that has demand not only in India, but in other countries as well. In the manufacturing and service sectors there are hundreds of skills and vocations for which there is a worldwide shortage. For example: automobile repair and service, TV, electrical appliance repair and service, medical and health services, nursing, and many others. India requires millions of trained people in 1000 other service areas and hundreds of skills for the manufacturing sector (there are 2500 trade options in Germany). India must reduce unemployment by supplying world class skilled people that are required by the nation and for rest of the world. The country must be run with higher efficiency, lesser wastage and lower cost of operation by providing vocational training.

There should be plenty of opportunities in the villages and in hubs of villages in the new towns and mini-new cities. Many people don't want to move out of their villages and leave their parents alone. Instead there should be more opportunities created in the rural areas. Here students can go through courses that can later land them in jobs or they can set up a small scale industry by themselves near their villages in mini-new cities.

Making the local community self-reliant should be the main focus of these programs. ITI courses should be conducted for 8th pass students in the field of home appliances repairs and maintenance, electrical motor winding, welding and hundreds of other courses. These courses will make them less dependent on agriculture for their living. With 70% of the Indian population living in rural areas there is huge potential of manpower waiting to be tapped.

Vocational training with apprenticeship in companies

In Germany a law was passed in 1969 which regulated and unified the vocational training system and codified the shared responsibility of the state, the unions, associations and chambers of trade and industry. The system is very popular in modern Germany. In 2001, approximately 51% of all young people under 22 completed an apprenticeship. One in three companies offered apprenticeships in 2003; in 2004 the government signed a pledge with industrial unions that all companies (excluding very small businesses) must take on apprentices.

This way, the business and trade receive low cost manpower for two to four years, while the youth are learning a new trade, both on-the-job as well as, learning theory in the Vocational Training Institutes. This combination produces youths with world-class skills. There are 2500 trade options in Germany. These vocations cover the manufacturing and service sectors as well as the New Economy, especially IT and renewable energy like solar and wind energy.

After standard ten, 80% to 90% of the youth in Russia opt for vocational training where they work part time (at minimum wages), as apprentices, with industry and trade for two to four years and study simultaneously in a Vocational Training Institute, for learning the theory and acquiring the relevant working knowledge and experience to be successful in the field.

The Asian Development Bank (ADB) has approved a $50 million loan for the Ministry of Education of Bangladesh to make its technical and vocational education and training (TVET) programs market-oriented, short-term, and relevant, especially for the poor who were not able to finish Grade 8. The Asian Development Bank (ADB) is helping thousands of unemployed and underemployed Bangladesh adults attain better wage and employment prospects by improving the country's technical skills training system.

The project supports the government's plan to reduce poverty and promote economic growth by providing market-relevant skills training to more Bangladeshis. Under the project, leaders of the ready-made garments and textiles, light engineering, and construction industries – the three main employers in the country – will help create skills training programs relevant to their industries.

Employment with vocational training

In India, vocational training program will help thousands of unemployed and underemployed adults attain better wage and employment prospects. The Vocational Education System will increase job prospects. Multinational companies will pour billions into the Indian economy, provided they are welcomed into India (the same way as China does). They will take advantage of the country's cheap labor and potentially the world's huge market. These companies will recruit local manpower and will impart intensive training to them.

The Chinese government has introduced the system of paying attention both to school diplomas and professional qualification certificates, trying many ways to promote various kinds of educational and training programs to improve the comprehensive capacity of working age people to obtain employment, to start a business or to adapt to occupational

Vocational Training

changes. Vocational training in China includes pre-employment training, apprentice training and on-the-job training, covering elementary, intermediary, and advanced vocational qualification training for technicians and other types of training to help people adapt to different job requirements.

In China emphasis lies in training new techniques, materials, technology and equipment to meet the urgent needs of enterprises for people with specialized skills and techniques. Multi-skilled talents, and people with both the needed knowledge and skills for the development of new and high technology. In China skilled workers are available in abundance, which is attracting capital and industry from all over the world. In the last decade they have improved their labor-intensive industries to more sophisticated industries.

The Bangladesh Vocational Education System is increasing Bangladesh job prospects. The Japanese textile titan, Toray Group, will pour around US$ 200 million into Bangladesh's textile sector. They are taking advantage of the country's cheap labor and potentially the world's hugest apparel market. The Japanese company's investment plan reflects Bangladesh's competitiveness in the textile industry, driven mainly by cheap labor. Toray has already recruited some local manpower and is imparting intensive training to them.

Toray's relocation move is thought to be part of the global change in businesses seeking low-cost manufacturing bases. Cheap labor is not the only factor that encouraged the Toray Group to invest in the country, rather Bangladesh's globally-competitive textile and apparel industry acted as an added incentive. Perhaps, they (Toray) will want to capitalize on the country's longstanding expertise in apparel and textiles. As the wage costs in Malaysia are sky rocketing, the foreign manufacturing companies will be relocating their factories in low-cost countries in the region, such as Bangladesh.

Current issues and trends in Technical and Vocational Education

Some countries reported special measures taken to promote rural development by providing special vocational courses for the rural population. During the dry season, special courses are arranged for the rural population through correspondence and evening courses. Finland for example endeavors to provide educational services using distance education for rural people who are unable to attend classes due to distance or other constraints.

In China, agricultural education plays a very important role for the accelerated rural development through the application of the special plan. Emphasis is laid on the modernization of rural agriculture. Rural schools are closely linked with local communities and are directly

Vocational Training

involved in rural development projects, responding to their needs.

In Fiji, the technical and vocational education contributes to the rural development by training students in rural areas for self-employment. Thus, students are taught essential life skills. In Germany, there are one-year technical colleges in agriculture and rural home economics to train future farm managers.

In India, the recent government policy is to develop technologies appropriate to and adaptable with the needs of rural, informal and other unorganized sectors. A very popular program, launched by the Community Polytechnics, is called 'Training of Rural Youth for Self-employment' (TRYSEM), aimed particularly at training school dropouts and some adults living in rural and remote areas. But this program and other programs cover a very small number of people in India, a fraction of China's programs.

In almost all countries, technical and vocational education is seen as a means of human resource development, leading to social and economic progress. Technical and vocational education has become a vital part of the education system. Many countries recognize the need to introduce various forms of continuing education, since full-time training cannot provide all required skills and knowledge to meet the developmental needs. Rapid technological advances in the past decade have further increased the need for relevant training and retraining programs. China's leaders are much more focused than their Indian counterpart on how to train their young people in maths, science, computers and other vocational skills required for success in the business world. This creates incentives that will attract global investors in industry and services. What is really necessary is for the people to wake up to the fact that there is a fundamental shift happening in the way people are doing business. As a nation India must improve to be able to compete. It is just going to be one global market.

Cheaper labour costs in manufacturing with vocational training

India can have prices as low as the Chinese, if India trains its rural people through education and vocational training. Even lots of rural Grade 5 drop-outs can be given vocational training; these students can be involved in manufacturing. This is the only way to begin to catch up with China in manufacturing. Indian companies in public sector and private sector industries should be given incentive to start new factories in these rural areas. Mini-new cities in the hub of villages, and SEZ should be developed in the heart of villages.

On-the-job training in manufacturing industries

In rural India 50% of the youth, after Standard 8, should opt for vocational training where they work part

Vocational Training

time (at minimum wages), as apprentices, with industry and trade for two to four years. They will study simultaneously in a Vocational Training Institute (part-time), for learning the theory and acquiring the relevant knowledge. This way, the business and trade receive low cost manpower for two to four years, while the youth are learning a new trade, both on-the-job as well as theory in the Vocational Training Institute. This combination will produce youth with world-class skills. These vocations will cover the manufacturing and service sectors as well as the new economy, especially IT and renewable energy like solar and wind energy. These types of programs will attract local and foreign industries to the mini-new Indian cities in the hubs of villages. This type of training will attract industries, especially labor intensive industries to the rural areas. These types of apprentice programs in vocational training are very popular in Germany and Russia.

What has been peculiar about India's development so far is that high growth has not been accompanied by a labor-intensive industrial revolution that could transform the lives of the hundreds of millions of Indians still trapped in rural poverty. Many Indians watch mesmerized as China seems to create an endless flow of low-end manufacturing jobs by exporting goods such as toys, electrical goods sanitary fittings and clothes. While China's better educated compatriots export knowledge services and manufacturing to the rest of the world. Economies in the rest of the world have evolved from agriculture to industry to service. India appears to have a weak middle step. Their industry's share is only at 26% as compared to 46% in China.

If India wants to benefit from the flattening of the world and interconnecting of the market and knowledge center, they will have to run as fast as China. In the future, globalization is going to be increasingly driven by the countries who adapt quickly to its process and technologies. The winners will be those who learn the process and skills most quickly. Many countries have leap frogged right into new technology without having to worry about the sunken costs of the old system. This means that they can move very fast to adapt new, state-of-the-art technology through vocational training.

India needs thousands of labor-intensive industries in the hubs of villages and especially poor villages where people can be employed by these industries. Labor-intensive industries can be found in hundreds of sectors. Few of them are textile, leather, electrical goods, castings and many more. Other areas are rebuilding and upgrading some areas of railways (old fossil fuel consuming engines, improving railway tracks for fast moving trains), old cars and buses to make them environmentally friendly. This can be done in the mini-new cities in the hub of villages; SEZ (Special Economic Zones) should be developed in the heart of village clusters.

Textile and apparel are labor-intensive industries.

Vocational Training

Millions more people can be employed by these industries. It has created an immense opportunity for India. It has strong potential from labor-intensive to more highly automated production. India cannot benefit only from present demands, but must prepare itself for the higher end of the market. In addition to the lower end, India can be a supplier to upper end manufacturing.

If India is alert enough and get its act together, it can take major advantage of the newly emerging opportunities and even make up for the ones missed earlier. India needs to act on this front speedily. The country cannot afford to forget a large number of small and tiny manufacturing units which are in the unorganized and the informal sector. Many plastic products, textile, leather and electrical goods are also manufactured by small and medium-sized industries. Indian rural people have the urge and the willingness to work hard. Due to lack of education and skill development opportunities, they are unable to utilize the available opportunities for better employment or to improve their standard of living. India needs to create clusters of villages or mini-new cities to provide quality centres of education and vocational training. People can easily commute between the villages and cluster of villages or mini-new cities to acquire the best skills and education.

Summary

India does not spend a sufficient amount of money

training its technical students to make India a manufacturing hub. Vocational education and training hardly exists in India, while China's number far exceeds that of India. India requires vocational training programs to prepare the youth for a vocation of their choice. Apprentice (vocational) training in Germany is considered one of the best in the world.

The vocational education system will increase job prospects. Vocational training in China includes pre-employment training, apprentice training and on-the-job training, covering elementary, intermediary, and advanced vocational qualification training for technicians and other types of training to help people adapt to different job requirements.

India can have prices as low as the Chinese, if India trains its rural people through education and vocational training. This type of training will attract industries, especially labour intensive industries to the rural areas.

General vocational training classes should be started in schools as a part of the curriculum because a large number of students will drop out at the primary level. Once a week, classes should be devoted to vocational training.

Indian vocational training for drop out students should be of short durations (say for three to six months). Let us build this system from the ground up on a very large scale.

Vocational Training

India requires vocational training programs to prepare the youth for a vocation of their choice. India should build up a large workforce that will have demand not only in India but in other countries as well. In the manufacturing and service sectors there are hundreds of skills and vocations for which there is a worldwide shortage.

Renewable Energy

India At The Crossroads

The area covered by sea ice in the Arctic has continued to shrink for the fifth consecutive year, according to data released by US scientists. The current rate of shrinkage is calculated at 8% per decade. At this rate there may be no ice at all by the summer of 2060. The result of melting of most of the Himalayan glaciers by 2030, as predicted by the UN panel on climate change, could be truly catastrophic for India, China and its neighbors. (Although some sources predict that these Himalayan glaciers could last till 2050).

The Himalayan glaciers are the largest store of water outside the polar ice caps, and feed seven great Asians rivers – Ganga, Indus, Brahmaputra, Mekong, Salween, Yangtze, Huang Ho (Yellow River). The first danger of the meltdown could be widespread flooding. In a few decades, it could be followed by irreversible droughts, threatening the livelihood of millions of people. This would not only mean unprecedented food shortages but also a massive water crisis.

Glaciers are not providing the snow melt they once did

Farmers all over the world have come to depend on glaciers to feed their rivers and drive their hydroelectric dams. But with temperatures rising, and a shorter winter, the glaciers are not providing the snowmelt they once did. China has been taking care of this by having a very large industrial base and consistently increasing the use of solar and wind energy in remote places. They have a very big surplus of industrial goods export -- and if needed, they can import food supplies with part of that money. India and China are having a short sighted policy, without realizing that once these glaciers are gone, which is predicted by 2030, they will be gone forever. Hundreds of millions of people rely on these glaciers and therefore drastic measures must be undertaken to save the glaciers.

By 2050 solar, wind, biomass and geothermal power could end USA, dependence on foreign oil and slash greenhouse gas emission. This will occur throughout the world, including China and India. In the meantime, power plants that burn coal, oil and natural gas, as well as vehicles everywhere, continue to pour millions of tons of pollutants and greenhouse gases into the atmosphere annually, threatening the planet. By that time the Himalayan glaciers will have permanently disappeared, affecting the lives of millions of people in India and China. By 2050 the population of India is predicted to be around two billion people. Meanwhile, China with its one child policy per family in place will be around one billion.

Climate change will have very devastating effects. It will lead to systematic changes in rainfall, evaporation, and river flow. Rising temperatures will accelerate the melting of glaciers and snow in the high mountains. Hundreds of millions of people depend on snowmelt and glacier melting for their water supply. This (rising temperature and climate change) will greatly threaten these vast areas. For some decades, the communities will be threatened by flooding caused by rapid glacier melting, but after that the risk will switch abruptly to water scarcity when the glaciers disappear altogether. Snowmelt will come earlier in the spring only and not be available during the dry summer months when crops require water for irrigation; when water is required the most.

As high temperatures increase, India and the rest of the world will see storms of increased intensity. The dry lands will become even drier. The frequency of droughts will rise significantly. The populous regions with water supplies dependent on annual snowmelt and long-term glacier melt will lose water security with the disappearance of the glaciers.

Falling water tables in wells

Indian farmers drilling millions of pump-operated wells in an ever-deeper search for water, threaten to suck the continent's under-ground reserves dry. The country that will be affected the most is India. Small farmers have abandoned traditional shallow wells where bullocks draw water in leather buckets, to drill 21 million tube wells and bore wells hundreds of yards below the surface, using technology adapted from the oil industry.

While the electric pumps have brought short-term prosperity to many and helped make India a major rice exporter in less than a generation, future implications are dire. So much water is being drawn from underground reserves that the pumps are running dry. Thus, they are turning fields that have been green for generations, into a desert. There has been no control over the expansion of pumps and wells. When the balloon bursts, untold anarchy will hit much of rural India.

Indian farmers were taking 200 cubic kilometers of water out of the earth each year, with only a fraction of that replaced by the monsoon rains. In northern China's plain, 30 cubic kilometers more water is pumped to the surface each year than is replaced by rain. Water shortage will soon make India and China dependent on grain imports.

Use of solar and wind energy for producing electricity

In some of the Indian villages, free electricity is available to rich farmers. These farmers have invested billions of Rupees in the new pumps, but they constantly have to drill deeper to keep pace with falling water tables. Half of India's traditional hand-dug wells and millions of shallow tube wells have already dried up, bringing a spate of suicides among those who rely on them. (Richer farmers are drilling tube wells hundreds of yards below the surface, using

Renewable Energy

technology adapted from the oil industry. Thus taking away water from small farmers (their neighbours) who are using traditional shallow wells, where bullocks draw water in leather buckets). Another consequence is a shortage in electricity, reaching epidemic proportions in some Indian states, where half of the power is used to pump water from up to a kilometer down.

There have been many warning signs that India has entered a new era in climate change. Scientists point to new data which is an indication of change in the average global temperature, rising sea level, and quickening glacial melt, drought like conditions and shortage of water and electricity. In India these conditions have been known to the central and state governments for the last 20 to 25 years or more, but nothing was been done about it.

By using alternative sources of energy India will not only improve pollution control and climate change but will also drastically cut the imports of petrol and oils. Fortunately, at this point in time, there is no need to reinvent the wheel on solar, wind energy, hybrid, and fuel cell technologies. The Central government must invest a substantial amount of money, but the payoff far exceeds the cost. Solar plants consume little or no fuel, saving billions of dollars year after year. With the economies of scale, the cost will decrease considerably. Moreover, solar systems can be manufactured and installed at a much faster rate than conventional power plants. This is because of their straightforward design and relative lack of environmental and safety complications.

Solar energy should especially be used in remote places and villages. If private enterprises do not see this benefit or cannot manufacture appliances for using solar energy, many government enterprises can utilize their resources to utilize solar power and inverters. This cannot be done until more private companies and foreign companies see the benefit and profit of manufacturing bulk solar energy utilization equipment -- and want to take part in it. India can be a leader in the field of alternative sources of energy. This is India's opportunity to affect such changes and become the leader in manufacturing solar panels and wind turbines. India can become the biggest user of solar power as well as be the world leader in the use of alternative source of energy.

There is an extensive range of applications where the solar photovoltaic (PV) system is already viewed as the best economical option for electricity supply. These systems are reliable and require little attendance and maintenance. These advantages render solar photovoltaic (PV) as the greatest opportunity for generating electricity for billions of people throughout the world, who are without electricity. In rural India alone, approximately 350 million people do not have electricity. These rural

Renewable Energy

people would greatly benefit from the use of solar and wind energy.

Large-scale use of clean energy technology would not only reduce pollution, but would create millions of good jobs and provide struggling communities around the world with a way out of poverty. Renewable energy, especially solar and wind generation, create far more jobs per unit of energy produced and per dollar spent than fossil fuel generation does. These methods of producing an abundance of electricity with solar and wind energy, will lead to the production of hydrogen fuel cells once that technology is perfected.

New challenges always present new opportunities. The most significant and positive factor in India's and China's favor is their size. The cost will continue to decline as the volume of solar panels and wind turbines production increases. Given India's and China's enormous population, the number of solar panels and wind turbines required would be high and therefore bring the cost per watt down significantly. Around the world, especially in Germany, Spain and Denmark, which are quite ahead of others in the production and use of solar panels and wind turbines, the prices will come down considerably.

India faces power failure on a daily basis, therefore most houses have installed invertors with batteries, especially in urban areas. When the power is off these inverters are used, and when the power is on again, electricity is used to recharge the batteries.

The rest of the time the inverters are not in use. By installing solar inverters instead of battery inverters, electricity will be free as long as the sun shines. Therefore, a significant amount of national money will be saved on electric bills. In rural areas, the additional advantage will be cheaper labor costs for maintenance and repair.

Next great industry - clean power and energy efficiency tools

India can produce numerous clean power and energy efficiency tools to be sold throughout the world as well as used within the country. India and China can get at least a three to five year jump on the next great global industry. India has a very big market for solar and wind power, especially in villages where there is no electricity. The additional advantage Indians would benefit from is when lots of people sell at least half of their electricity produced by solar and wind to the national grid. This could be a source of income for millions of poor people. At the moment, solar and wind energy equipment are in short supply throughout the world. Our public sector units have the base for manufacturing, the ability to raise huge volumes of low interest capital from the banks and cheap labor available to them in rural areas, to produce solar and wind energy equipment and energy efficiency tools. This industry sector will become much bigger than the telephone and IT industry in India now has.

Rural poverty can be reduced with electricity use

It is not just lack of money that keeps the poor mired in poverty -- it is also the lack of access to energy. In Indian villages people use mostly charcoal, crop residues, and cow dung, usually in a way that is harmful to both our health and the environment. Many of the world's poor earn one dollar a day and can't afford to pay for solar panels, therefore subsidies are clearly required. Electricity can transform remote villages, helping them leapfrog from the Dark Ages to the twenty-first century. Experts say that local entrepreneurs can turn to profit by leasing out a small 35 KW solar unit, which is enough to power two bulbs and a radio for just $75 a year.

Electricity can have a dramatic impact on education and literacy. Children can study at night after they have completed their chores, which will help increase academic success, leading to better future job prospects. If India is to have any hope of lifting the yoke of absolute poverty, it must provide rural villages with greater access to electricity. The rich world should help the developing countries utilize clean energy. Unless rich countries help poor countries to leapfrog over the dirtiest energy phases that the rich world experienced, the future for all may be needlessly grim.

Fortunately, the current president of the United

States, Barack Obama is for clean energy technology. Decisions taken in the next few years about energy in the US will shape the investments made in energy infrastructure for at least a generation. If micro power really takes off, then there is every reason for optimism about our planet's future.

Wind and solar technologies are already cost-effective today. Simply breaking down the market barriers to their deployment would have a much bigger impact now. Action taken by the United States will be felt all over the world. Revolution will come with clean, abundant, cheap, reliable energy through a smarter grid.

Government mandatory policies needed to promote renewable energy

Huge demand must be created for existing clean power technologies in USA and Europe, like wind and solar, in order to reduce the cost of these technologies and make them competitive with conventional fossil fuels. Already existing clean power technologies can be made much cheaper and more effective today with the set of government policies.

The only way to change the situation and set off the forest fire of innovation in energy that is needed, is to reshape the market in a way that will make it much easier for clean power technologies to compete with and challenge the presently used fossil fuels. The way to do that is with taxes and incentives that will stimulate huge demand for clean power technologies that already exist, like wind and solar. This will stimulate more research and development by private companies and universities. In the end we will transform our economy and save ourselves from so many other problems in the process.

An effective price signal would be a national renewable energy mandate. Such a mandate would tell power companies that by a certain date, say 2015, they would have to generate 20% of their power from renewable energy by law: solar photo voltaic, solar thermal, hydro, wind, or any other clean process. A renewable mandate such as this would stimulate massive amounts of innovation.

In countries such as Denmark, Spain and Germany, imposed portfolio standards are for wind power on their utilities, requiring them to produce a certain amount each year and offer long-term subsidies. This created a big market for wind-turbine manufacturers in Europe in the 1980s. You have to build on the certainty that the demand is going to be there. Companies throughout the world will take the technical risk; they will find technological breakthroughs. But they must know that if huge investments are made, there is a $100 billion national and international market that they can step into.

The Indian government is planning to buy 6 to 10 nuclear plants. The cost could be $15 billion to $20 billion. The completion of plants may take 8 to 10 years which does not present a problem. However, India should spend $50 billion on solar and wind energy in next five years, in order to create tens of millions of jobs and countless new industries that will arise from this. With electricity in villages, students will be able to study at night and as a result, their education and livelihood can be drastically improved. The payback in terms of benefits period will begin from the very first year this is put into effect.

Massive wastage and theft in power transmission

The world's system of electricity has evolved as a hugely centralized system, in which power is generated at distant locations and then shipped through an elaborate transmission and distribution system of heavy-duty wires, transformer stations, before reaching our homes and offices. This system has lot of wastage and theft in India. The electricity board transmission and distribution losses amounted to about 30% to 40%. Much of this is outright theft. Billions of dollars have been wasted by giving free electricity to politically important groups, such as rich farmers. All this has been a recipe for disaster.

Dramatic advances in software and electronics offer new and more flexible ways to link parts of electrical systems together. The power plants are now selling power to the grid as well as buying from it in the USA and Europe.

Renewable Energy

The coming energy revolution could be bigger than the telecommunication revolution because it is the world's biggest industry and therefore will drastically impact our environment.

Each manufacturer of cars in India can be persuaded to bring few models each powered by an alternative source of energy. Be it in electric, hybrid, fuel cells or solar technology. An incentive can be given to these manufacturers by buying new technology cars for staff of the different levels of Governments and give them some tax break. Electric buses can also be bought by municipal governments.

India can turn disadvantages into advantages by converting three-wheelers, buses and older model cars to electric cars. The West won't adopt this technology for a few years to come as many people believe things are going back a few years. While in India, with different modes of transportation, converting used vehicles to electric cars will be a step forward.

India has another advantage over many other countries. For converting three-wheeler scooters, buses, old cars lots of professional Engineers are required as this conversion could be dangerous, without the proper supervision of professionals. These conversions can take place in municipal garages, central government garages, state government garages and public undertakings, where spare capacity is available. Some car manufacturers can also be persuaded or given some sort of incentive to do this type of conversion and of course small scale industries will generate millions of jobs in this venture.

Fuel-cell power plants are moving from theory to reality. This will leapfrog the current hybrid technology. The vehicle would be powered by gasoline, diesel fuels or hydrogen fuel-cell. Toyota has a decade-long lead in selling more than one million gasoline-electric cars.

The Toyota Prius hybrid car is a perfect example of a new system replacing an old one and creating a whole new function. The Prius is not a better car, it is a better system! What is new about the Prius is that its designers looked at it as a system that could perform more than one function. They use the energy from braking to generate electricity so that the battery can be recharged and used for driving as many miles as possible, instead of using the gasoline in the tank. The kinetic energy created by the spinning of the wheels is stored in the battery and reused.

RailPower of Canada created a hybrid locomotive that could provide plenty of oomph (energy) to move railway wagons and coaches around without wasting fuel. It is like hybrid engines in cars – vehicles like Toyota Prius that run on a combination of gas, electricity and re-chargeable batteries. The whole world should cooperate and sell these technologies to each other.

Renewable Energy

Latest technology needed for new and refurbished locomotives

To start with, India needs to refurbish its existing locomotives and import new ones and also manufacture with the latest technology. The combined efforts will have great synergy. Moreover, to expedite the process, a lot of refurbishing work can be done in the private sector and by small scale industries. India needs a central authority which could decide and coordinate quickly, when to import the energy efficient locomotives and keep on importing new and efficient technology for railways.

China has been buying large numbers of big GE OL' locomotive engines made in Erie, Pennsylvania (USA). These huge GE industrial sized diesel engines pull long trains. Although China manufactures diesel engine locomotive, they prefer to buy these locomotives from the USA -- because of obvious advantages, including fuel efficiency. These high standards helped to drive the innovation of a big train engine that spewed out less pollution, while also increasing fuel economy and thereby lowering CO_2 emissions in the process.

GE Transportation will have exported about three hundred of these to China by the end of 2009. Also, they will be sold to railroad companies worldwide, including in Mexico, Brazil, Australia, and Kazakhstan. One would wonder why a country like China which makes its own much cheaper locomotive, thousands of them in fact would buy from General Electric. GE's are the most energy efficient in the world, with the lowest emissions of CO_2. This is the reason China buys them. The EVO's new twelve-cylinder engine produces the same horsepower as its sixteen-cylinder predecessor. Best of all, these locomotives are very efficient and reliable.

High powered long haul electric locomotives

India has great scope for deploying more high powered electric locomotives. In addition to the electricity produced by the usual methods, India can produce solar and wind energy on vast stretches of land owned by Indian railways. Indian railways can also buy solar and wind energy produced by rural people. Lots of Indians would benefit when they sell at least half their electricity produced by solar and wind energy generated installations, to the national grid (for electric locomotives). This could be a source of income for millions of people. Our public sector units have the base for manufacturing wind and solar energy equipment, which can be used by railways and others. Unlike the Amtrak in USA and Canadian Pacific railways that traverse huge tracts of wide open unpopulated spaces travelled nonstop, Indian railway network has many railway stations (stops). This can be used as an advantage and Indian railways can move up from diesel locomotives to electric traction even for long distance transit.

India needs hundreds of cellulosic ethanol plants

close to big cities near waste sites. The plants where ethanol is made from waste or switch grass and not from food crops. These are multiyear investments and cost billions of dollars. Along with governments, multinational companies will invest in these projects if they have some certainty on the incentives and on the market side. In India, ethanol is made from molasses left after making sugar. There are other proposals and potential of saving foreign exchange, generating jobs, using arid and wasteland productively and controlling carbon dioxide emissions.

The first phase of the ethanol-blended petrol was to launch in January 2003, but it has taken the industry a good three years to iron out start-up glitches. One issue has been that ethanol imported from Brazil was available at a lower price than domestic ethanol. This Brazilian ethanol prices vary according to their demand and supply position. To encourage domestic industry of ethanol making, we should fix a floor price adding an import duty or taxes when needed. Otherwise Indian ethanol production will shut down, once the low priced Brazilian ethanol is available in the market.

Electricity will transform the quality of life in rural India

Solar power will help develop cottage industries in villages and mini-new cities. Cheap trained labour in remote villages will develop clothing industries and many other cottage industries. If we want to compete with China, we will have to train and educate millions of people in villages. The industry will move in those areas where there is electricity, trained labour and other infrastructures available. Many people will ultimately establish their own small businesses in villages or in mini-new cities where electricity becomes available.

Renewable energy is affordable

For many people living in rural areas in India, clean or renewable energy is seen as unaffordable and out-of-reach in practical terms. However, for the last few years, a project piloted by the United Nations Environment Programme (UNEP) is attempting to change that perception by bringing solar power to rural mainstream India through micro-financing. The project has already reached approximately 100,000 people, including those in the state of Karnataka, saving money in the long-term and transforming the quality of life for many.

The UNEP estimates that a single wick of kerosene for indoor lighting can burn up to 80 liters (21 gallons) of fuel, emitting more than 250 kilograms (551 pounds) of carbon dioxide per year. Not to mention the fact that in developing countries, 64% of deaths and 81% of lifelong disabilities in children, younger than five years, is directly attributed to the use of these inefficient and "dirty" fuels.

It is no surprise then, that the UNEP's $1.5 million solar Home project to distribute solar photovoltaic (PV) kits is such a success. Currently, the greatest obstacle for solar power to get a foothold in this market has been mostly due to lack of financing for clean energy in rural communities. However, by initially teaming up with two large Indian banks, the kits were made affordable through low-interest loans of $300-500, to be repaid over five years. In addition to the loans, the banks organized a vendor qualification process that resulted in five solar vendors offering their services and giving customers more flexibility to choose from. With small bank loans in place, the possibility for usage of solar power in Indian rural areas is tremendous.

Summary

The result of the melting of most of the Himalayan glaciers by 2030, as predicted by the UN panel on climate change, could be truly catastrophic for India, China and its neighbors. Water shortage will soon make India and China dependent on grain imports.

In a few decades, it could be followed by irreversible droughts, threatening the livelihood of millions of people. This would not only mean unprecedented food shortages but also a massive water crisis.

So much water is being drawn from underground

reserves that the electric pumps are running dry, turning fields that have been green for generations into a desert.

Solar energy should especially be used in remote places and villages. In rural India approximately 350 million people do not have electricity. Large-scale use of clean energy technology would not only reduce pollution, but would create millions of good jobs.

The cost will continue to decline as the volume of solar panels and wind turbines production increases. Given India's and China's enormous population, the number of solar panels and wind turbines required would be high and therefore would bring the cost per watt down significantly.

Currently, solar and wind energy equipment are in short supply throughout the world. Our public sector units have the base of manufacturing, the ability to raise huge volumes of low interest from the banks and cheap labour is available to them in rural areas to produce solar and wind energy equipment and energy efficiency tools.

This industry and sector will become much bigger than the telephone and IT industry India now possesses. If private enterprises do not see this benefit or cannot manufacture solar energy as needed, many government enterprises (public sector manufacturing units) can utilize their resources to manufacture solar power generation panels, inverters

Renewable Energy

and wind turbines.

Electricity can transform remote villages, helping them leapfrog from the Dark Ages to the twenty-first century. Experts say that local entrepreneurs can turn a profit by leasing out a small 35 KW solar unit, which is enough to power two bulbs and a radio for just $75 a year.

Electricity can have a dramatic impact on education and literacy. Children can study at night after they have completed their chores. This will help increase academic success, leading to better future job prospects. If India is to have any hope of lifting the yoke of absolute poverty, it must provide rural villages with greater access to electricity.

The rich world should help the developing countries to use clean energy. Unless rich countries help poor countries to leapfrog over the dirtiest energy phases that the rich world experienced, the future for all may be needlessly grim.

The world already has a huge demand for solar and wind energy. These existing clean power technologies can be made much cheaper and more effective today with the set of government policies, tax incentives, and regulations. With innovation, solar light will eventually be at a cost below that of coal-power.

India should spend $50 billion on solar and wind energy (in next five to ten years) in order to create tens of millions of jobs -- and countless new industries will arise from this. With this investment, hundreds of alternative source of energy manufacturers will come to India with capital and the latest technology. The payback in terms of direct benefits period will begin from the very first year this is put into effect.

Creation of new towns

India At The Crossroads

Creation of new towns

India was featured on the cover of a recent issue of Business Week. This is what Business Week had to say:

[India's] infrastructure deficit is so critical that it could prevent India from achieving the prosperity that finally seems to be within its grasp. Without reliable power and water and a modern transportation network, the chasm between India's moneyed elite and its 800 million poor will continue to widen, potentially destabilizing the country.

The infrastructure deficit is so critical and unless the nation begins a drastic overhaul of the existing order and overcomes the legacy of corruption, politics and bureaucracy, its ability to build adequate infrastructure will remain in doubt. So will its economic destiny.

Even with 10% economic growth, the benefits will not be inclusive and won't be fast enough to filter down to all sections of the population. We have to think of measures to improve income per head in the rural non-agriculture sector. The poor state of infrastructure is the biggest obstacle to growth and requires major improvement.

India needs reconstruction initiative like Marshall Plan in post war West Europe

This is the time for efforts on the scale of the Marshall Plan: to improve the infrastructure of the country. A "Marshall Plan" was put together by the US at the end of the Second World War, for the reconstruction of Western Europe. By aiding in the reconstruction, the US helped build capacity in Europe. A side-effect of this was increased employment for Americans within the United States to supply the goods that Europe required. Once Europe regained its economy, it was a ready market for American goods and services, and became their biggest trading partner. India needs a reconstruction effort similar to that of the Marshall Plan, where urban India helps to construct rural India. As rural India regains its economy, it will become a ready market for urban goods and services and will become successful trading partners.

At this critical moment there is a dire need to massively improve India's infrastructure. During the time of recession, the huge underground train system in London was built. In the United States, Tennesse Valley Authority in the 1930's, at the time of profound economic crisis, created millions of jobs. In addition to fighting poverty, it provided infrastructure including a large network of dams, electricity, and waterways for navigation. Currently there is a recession throughout the world. In spite of the recession, there is an opportunity to build new cities. USA is allocating $600 billion to improve their economy. China is putting $580 billion towards improving the infrastructure of the country in the next two years. This is in addition

Creation of new towns

to the huge amount China has already invested. India should put forth $400 to $500 billion in the Public and Private sectors towards: infrastructure, Microloans, schools (including vocational schools and colleges), seed money towards building mini-new cities in the midst of villages in the next three years.

In Tech Talk: Creating India's New Cities: Think Big written by Atanu Dey and Rajesh Jain, they discuss in their article series how the big changes are easier to accomplish than small changes. They also discuss the condition of the big existing cities which are dying. Atanu Dey writes:

> There is something in the nature of the world that it is sometimes paradoxically more difficult to make small changes than to make big changes. Logically, consistent big changes are more likely to succeed because of the interconnectedness of the world. India was forced to liberalize its economy when the external shock to the system arrived in the form of an external balance of payment crisis

> The existing cities are dying and although the situation within them is dire and unbearable, it is the result of continuous adjustment to gradually worsening conditions over a sufficiently long period. These cities will not collapse in the next few years but if present trends continue, in a decade or so, they will be dead. It is better to consider alternative plans

now rather than when the collapse eventually happens.

Half of the world's population, especially in the developed world lives in cities. The world's most developed regions: Europe and North America have far more people in cities than in the countryside. Currently, only 30% of India's population resides in cities. India needs at least 600 cities to populate the 600 million out of 900 million people that live in villages. Most of these cities should be situated an hour drive (or one to two hour bicycle ride) from the villages.

India should build hundreds of New Towns

India should build hundreds of new towns and base the economy of the towns on a combination of manufacturing, services and agriculture. The basic model is simple: a developer acquires a sufficiently large piece of non-agricultural, inexpensive land. The developer could be a public-private consortium who makes improvements on the land such as adding utility, roads and buildings. Then he proceeds to gain the interest of a few big commercial anchor tenants, to locate themselves on this land and sell or rent subdivisions to whosoever wants it. Once improvements on the land have begun and the work proceeds stage by stage, small bits are sold off to interested parties to pay for the on-going improvements on the land. An additional source of

Creation of new towns

financing could be long term bonds raised for initial investment for a mini-new city.

These anchor firms will expand their output since they anticipate that the economy will grow rapidly as new cities were being built. The demand for labor will go up. The labor will come primarily from the agricultural sector, and will become highly productive in non-agriculture sectors such as manufacturing and services. Even though the economy of the regions will grow at a very fast rate, there will be no inflation.

All sorts of service providers will move in, from schools to shopping, banks to bakeries. With sufficient income, the workers would be able to purchase the products of agriculture, manufacturing and service unit, there will be all round growth. Employed workers will use their income to buy food and housing. Apartments and houses will be available at very reasonable prices.

India needs a Marshall Plan where the urban part helps construct cities for the rural part. The result will be that the rural part will buy from urban India. Thus rural India will become a ready market for urban Indian goods and services and vice versa. With the growth of rural India, the per capita GDP will increase considerably in the next seven to ten years, placing India in the league of middle-income economies. Building new cities will transform population from 70% rural to 40% rural. Because of this, farm income will increase considerably. By organizing their resources and skills, the people of India will revolutionize their lives, and as a result, the economy will soar.

The success of the Chinese did not come without a vision and proper planning. They have a holistic view of planning. After being successful in one area, China quickly applies this success formula to the whole country. This is not true for India. China has replaced their members of communist parties with engineers and other qualified people from industries and businesses. China benefits from the most respected academics, successful entrepreneurs and business tycoons from China and across the world. They planned and decided which companies of the world to invite to China to do business. Foreign companies came to China with capital and foreign investment, technology and the US market. Chinese gave them land and other facilities to start their factories on war footing. They provided them with cheap skilled, semi-skilled and unskilled labor at almost one tenth of the cost of the US, with a promise of no labor strikes.

Similarly, foreign firms should be invited to India and offered all the facilities that China gives: tax benefits for ten years and no strikes for ten years. Foreign companies will come to India with capital or foreign investments, technologies and US and European markets. India should provide the companies with land and other facilities to start businesses on war footing. Similar facilities and terms should be

Creation of new towns

extended to local firms for their additional factories in the hub of rural areas in mini-new cities or special economic zones. In short, these foreign and Indian firms should be welcomed by local, state, and central governments.

To build new cities, India also needs a committee of experts from the industry and business sectors, as well as successful entrepreneurs and academics. India needs the best assistance from urban planning, finance, science, technology and management from both within the country, and the world, to give their recommendations and plans. Their goal is to build 600 cities, housing around a million people each, on average. The master plan we need should be a marvel of planning. Over the centuries, people have learnt a lot about how cities work and how to design them, so that they are comfortable for living and working in, as well as economically efficient.

Even during the best years, when economic growth was at 9% (now it is less), the benefits of that did not filter down to all sections of the population, especially to those in rural areas. Fast and inclusive growth should ensure that it reaches every part of the country. India should improve the productivity and income per head in the rural areas. Three-quarters of rural India should be engaged in the non-agriculture sector, such as industries and the service sector. The poor state of infrastructure is the biggest obstacle to growth and the system requires major improvements.

In addition to Bangalore, Delhi and Mumbai International companies are already getting involved in outsourcing from other cities, such as: Ahmadabad, Chennai, Hyderabad, Kochi, Kolkata, Mangalore, Nagpur, Pune, Thiruvanthapuram, Visakhapatnam and Chandigarh. Multinational and Indian companies will choose cities based on several factors including population, accessibility, educational level of the workforce, other infrastructure and existing companies who have businesses in these cities. India is a big country and more and more international companies may move their labor-intensive work to India in the next few years.

Farm labor is very low paying, seasonal work. Farm workers are forced to migrate to existing cities where there is no promise of jobs. They live in slums in the big cities and do not make sufficient money to return to their villages. Unfortunately so much money has been spent on the maintenance of the big cities, and yet the slums keep growing. Politicians of the city and the country, at the time of elections encourage people to live in parks and other open spaces, which is mostly government land (old monuments with open spaces are occupied by unscrupulous means), which ultimately become slums. Indian politicians use these people who live in slums as vote banks, unlike in other developed democracies. Ideally, some of these people seeking work will live in mini-new cities so that they can be near their villages. At the harvesting season, some of them can be easily available to work

Creation of new towns

as additional help to their families in the villages, or in the fields.

The words of the great visionary and urban planner, Daniel Burnham (1846 - 1912) states:

> Make no little plans. They have no magic to stir men's blood and probably themselves will not be realized. Think Big.

It is time to think big, because the Indian people have what it takes to make a big dream a reality. One such Indian example is the Nano car, which is a milestone because it is testimony to the fact that a world-class product can be conceived of and designed by Indian engineers and produced in India. Nano is the triumph of one man, Ratan Tata, the man who dreamt big. He is a leader of the team who visualized a product that never existed before.

Model city of Chandigarh

Another example of a big idea or dream is the Model city of Chandigarh. Capital of the state of Punjab and Haryana, Chandigarh is one of the most modern cities in India. Chandigarh, the first planned modern city of independent India was designed by the French architect Le Corbusier and its major work was completed by 1955. We need 600 mini-new cities with a little seed money from the central government, leaving the rest of the development to the private sector.

India At The Crossroads

Chandigarh, 250km north of Delhi, is one of the world's most distinctive and charming places. It has very well laid roads, lined with rows of trees. The city itself is very well planned and has beautiful buildings. Most of what is needed for daily living can be accessed on foot. There are many shops and essential services in each sector.

Chandigarh is full of parks and green spaces, quiet and fresh air and playgrounds for children. There are abundance of museums and colleges, and new jobs in the IT sector. The architecture is really neat and clean, with green space and buildings in balance. Outsiders would not believe that this beautiful setting is India.

Jawaharlal Nehru, the first prime minister of independent India, wanted a modern city (Chandigarh) which could ultimately become a model city for hundreds of future new cities. This city was designed for a population of up to 500,000, and is now home to double that or more. People are attracted to the city's standard of living where average incomes are quite high.

Chandigarh was an international effort to create a new kind of postcolonial city in India. People have been coming back from abroad to retire here. They have lived in cultured, ordered, clean societies. In keeping with that tradition there is a desire to keep the city spotless. It does not have the slums of Mumbai and Delhi. With the slums comes the segregation of

Creation of new towns

society. It also gives criminals a place to hide among good people. Lots of people lose their self-respect and many criminal gangs hire youngsters from the unemployed or under employed people to do their dirty jobs.

Indians in general are hardworking individuals who take on a lot of initiative and are full of ideas. However, it is unfortunate that in India people will start many projects, and once they succeed, the success formula is not applied to India as a whole. After independence, model cities like Chandigarh, Bhubaneshwar and Gandhinagar were built. With a little seed money from the central government, leaving the rest of the development to the private sector, hundreds of cities could have been built in the last 50 years in the hubs of villages.

After the success of Chandigarh, the central government could have spent only a fraction of the money to build these new cities. Very little money was needed to build other cities comparable to Chandigarh. Chandigarh was the capital of the state government and therefore needed to hold various government offices. This include a 10 storey secretariat building, government employees' houses, state assembly buildings, high court buildings, state university buildings and scores of other prominent buildings. Many people who came to India after partition made Chandigarh their home. Chandigarh was a dream city in the desert and a new beginning for many people in India.

India would be transformed by building new cities which are designed and built using the best planning principles and implementation. The master plan could be a marvel of urban planning, as is known in today's world. Differences in planning the layout between the model city of Chandigarh and other new cities would vary. The main difference perhaps in planning could be many high rise buildings, as compared to Chandigarh. Many people will live in very tall high-rise buildings, with the average residential building having around 20 stories. By living in high density high-rises, space is freed up within the city for more greenery and wider roads. The difference between now and when Chandigarh was built, is that the population of India has tripled in the last 60 years.

Another main difference will be the water supply. There is going to be tremendous shortage of water in India due to climate change, water tables in wells dropping and melting of glaciers. Planners will have to take this into consideration. Provision for large artificial bodies of water where rain water will be collected, as well as the recycling of water and waste will be necessary.

Most of the manufacturing and other such facilities that are not required to be within the city will be located in the outskirts. Renewable energy will be the main source of future energy. Cities will be designed in such a way to cut down needless driving around in order to avoid traffic problems. The planners and designers of the new city will have to keep the present conditions and some future projections in mind. For example, provisions for public transport including high speed trains.

New urban growth centers in hubs of village groupings

There is clearly a need to have new urban centers to accommodate the hundreds of millions of people who need to be in the cities for economic growth and development. Urbanization will help economic growth around the villages. In cities the infrastructure is less costly because of economies of scale. The cost will continue to decline as the volume produced increases. The high demand and supply of infrastructure in urban areas makes lower prices possible. Presently, almost all the major cities are little more than mega-slums. They are inadequate for the current residents, let alone adding hundreds of millions more people to them.

India has about 70% of its population, or 900 million people spread over 600,000 villages. India should develop say 600 mini-new cities to house about 1,000,000 people in the hubs of 600,000 small villages. These mini-new cities can then obtain the economics of scale normally associated with urban areas. Clearly there is no need to urbanize all the villages, however new cities in the hubs of the village groupings will be the best alternative. There is also no need for people to migrate to the existing mega cities, which are already bursting at the seams. New cities have to be planted for the hundreds of millions who are living in villages. This is the primary role of the government; with seed money from the government and the cooperation of the private sector, this can be made possible.

These mini-new cities should be chosen based on several factors: an existing or future railway station, existing roads and roads under construction, population, workforce and transportation. For now and for the near future of potential companies which will do business in these cities. The resources that are required will be created during the process of building the cities. Cities produce goods and services and that generates wealth which can be used to produce the cities that generate even more wealth.

New cities will be built from scratch for 600 million people. There is a scope to build houses, schools, shopping centers, parks, factories, roads, public utilities, hospitals, libraries, banks to bakeries. Today's urban planning is the best available known to humankind. Take whatever humanity knows about the best way to get things done, and use that to design and build cities that can develop and sustain the

Creation of new towns

people for generations. This is the greatest opportunity we have of building from scratch.

The government has to play the role of the "lead investor", signaling to the market that investment in the project will be profitable. The role of the government is one of financing the infrastructure, and encouraging further development by the private sector. Cities create wealth and that wealth is what creates cities.

It is possible to connect clusters of villages in such a way that movement from one village to another can be quick and convenient. Many agro industries, services industries and even high tech concerns can be relocated in such clusters of villages or mini-new cities by moving a few government offices and providing special concessions for industries. Once the process starts, economic activities will take care of the rest. These clusters of villages or mini-new cities have to be managed in an imaginative fashion, involving local people, panchayats, business persons and the intelligentsia, who will reside there. Some states have already shown interest in developing a few clusters into mini-new cities.

Modern rural India should have new cities consisting of an agrarian, industrial and service economy. These mini-new cities will have small, medium and large industries especially labour intensive industries, service centres, food processing sector, clothing industries and leather industries, which have colossal employment creating potential. There will also be schools, colleges, vocational training schools, hospitals in these cities. Almost 75% of the income in rural areas should come from non-agriculture sources. This means that three quarters of the agriculture households should be engaged in non-agricultural activities that will create jobs for hundreds of millions of people in rural area.

Need for creation of well-planned cities

It is astonishing that 2,600 years ago, when most of the world was living in tiny little human settlements, the Indus Valley civilization (India) had well-planned cities of Harappa and Mohenjo-Daro? Most of the current inhabitants of the land of Harappa and Mohenjo-Daro civilization live, not in well planned cities, but in tiny little impoverished villages, and some non-planned congested mega-slums. With slavery dating back for centuries, India has not only lost their spirit for building great cities but also lost the ability of thinking big.

A Wikipedia article on urban planning states:

> Some of these cities appear to have been built based on a well-developed plan. The streets of major cities such as Mohenjo-Daro and Harappa were paved and were laid out at right angles (and aligned north, south, east or west) in a grid pattern with a hierarchy of streets (commercial boulevards to small residential

Creation of new towns

alleyways), somewhat comparable to that of present day New York. The houses were protected from noise, odors, and thieves, and had their own wells, and sanitation. And the cities had drainage, large granaries, water tanks, and well-developed urban sanitation.

The world has moved on. They have built many wonderful cities. Our leaders refuse to dream for the country. They are too busy with their bickering over who gets how much of the material wealth. Leaders want more and more for themselves and for their parties. Not a single leader of India is calling for the creation of great well-planned, beautiful cities. If India utilizes its collective wisdom and skills, the people have the power to dream big.

With the growth of 600 well-planned cities, the demand for labor will go up. The labor for construction of the city, industries and businesses would come primarily from the agricultural sector, providing employment to the farms around the area. Even though the economy of the region would be growing at a very fast rate, there would be no inflation. India needs to shift its focus and encourage private capital to move from urban to rural areas, especially in the hub of villages and mini-new cities.

Summary

India needs a Marshall Plan effort, where urban India helps to construct rural India. Currently, only 30% of

India's population resides in cities. India needs a Marshall Plan where the urban part helps construct mini-new cities for the rural part.

Many high-rise buildings will be built in mini-new cities in the hubs of villages. India has about 70% (900 million people) spread over 600,000 villages. India needs at least 600 cities to provide for 600 million out of people that live in villages. Most of these cities should be situated an hour drive (or one to two hour bicycle ride) from the villages.

Chandigarh was built as the first modern city after India's independence. After the success of Chandigarh, the central government could have spent only a fraction of the money to build other mini-new cities.

India would be transformed by building new cities which are designed and built using the best planning and implementation strategies. Differences in planning the design between the model city of Chandigarh and other new cities would vary.

Even with 10% economic growth, the benefits will not be inclusive and won't be fast enough to filter down to all sections of the population. We have to think of measures to improve income per head in the rural non-agricultural sector. India's poor state of infrastructure is its biggest obstacle to growth and requires major improvement.

Creation of new towns

India should chip in $400 to $500 billion in the Public and Private sectors to put towards: infrastructure, schools (including vocational schools) and colleges. This would serve as seed money towards building mini-new cities in the midst of villages in the next three years.

India should build hundreds of new cities and base the economy of the city on a combination of manufacturing, service providing and agriculture. We need 600 new cities, with a little seed money from the central government, and leave rest of the development to the private sector.

These new cities should have nice apartment buildings that are well planned; roads lined with rows of trees. There should be lots of parks, green spaces and playgrounds for children. There should be many shops and self-sufficient local markets. Most of what is needed for daily living ought to accessed on foot.

India At The Crossroads

Second Green Revolution

Second Green Revolution

The food crisis is the result of increasing and growing consequences of neglect of agriculture in India. India needs a Second Green Revolution to address the problem of food security. Today India is in its greatest agrarian crisis since the eve of the Green Revolution. Farming and a falling water table have affected the productivity that gave rise to India's Green Revolution of the mid 1960s.

Using precision agricultural tools for modern farming is the key to increased output and profitability. In the light of lack of adequate funds, small farmers are still using traditional methods of farming. Microcredit should be provided for this purpose by the banks. Use of superior technology such as drip irrigation, water collection and precision application of fertilizers to obtain better output and higher profits is necessary. Special incentives should be provided for dry-land cultivation.

The effect of the agrarian crisis manifests itself in many ways. India has seen the lowest levels of growth in agricultural production in decades. For the first time the population growth rate has outstripped the agricultural production growth rate in decades. India is also dealing with the lowest levels of employment in rural India than has been seen in over a decade. Millions of people are migrating to towns and cities in search of jobs that don't exist.

It is becoming increasingly hard to make a living from wheat, a problem particularly acute in Haryana and Punjab, two states which alone account for 60% of India's wheat output. The water level has gone down and there is not enough water to irrigate the fields. Over farming and a falling water table, have affected productivity that gave rise to India's Green Revolution of the mid-1960s.

A Second Green revolution is needed to bridge the rural-urban divide and help turn India into a developed nation. Agriculture is pulling down the economy, which cannot be afforded since it is the largest employer in the country. A Second Green Revolution is necessary in light of the agriculture growth rate that has plummeted in the last few years. This is in spite of the fact that India has a competitive advantage in agriculture, with plenty of arable land, sunshine, and water. There could be a water shortage in the near future unless water is used conservatively, (more crop per drop of water).

The Western China Development Project, the world's largest regional development project, is spreading economic development in lagging regions in the interior since the year 2000. The Chinese government has invested more than $150 billion in Western China's development of infrastructure and environment conservation, mainly reforestation to help the western regions catch up. The results have been impressive: between 2000 and 2006, western China's production nearly doubled. Lots of jobs have been created in reforestation.

Encourage private capital to move from urban to rural areas

India needs to shift its focus from peasant farming to agribusiness, industry and encourage private capital to move from urban to rural areas. It would need to lift onerous distribution controls, allowing large retailers to contract directly from farmers, invest in irrigation, and permit the consolidation of fragmented holdings.

In the book *The Caged Phoenix,* Dipankar Gupta writes:

> It is fairly clear that if contract farming were made a viable option for small farmers, it would help them in a number of ways. To begin with, they can, as is done in Europe, lease out their holdings to big operators, use the income as a backup and move to urban centers. Second, once contract farming becomes a safe proposition, land that has remained fallow for want of cultivation can be put back into use. Third, as operations will now be at a much higher level, crop yields too will be greater and over time the small land owner can hope to earn higher returns from leasing out his land. Finally, if land records were to be maintained properly then that too would lend security to

small farmers and aid the cause of large-scale contract farming. Today records are often non-specific and are not all kept up-to-date and small farmers are afraid to leave their land for extended periods of time without leaving a relative or parent at home. This fear not only hinders mobility but also adds to the burden of maintaining uneconomic holdings. (page 128)

Farmers want the government to encourage the setting up of factories in towns near their villages in order to enable their children to earn a decent and regular income. Most villagers want to earn non-agricultural incomes. They want to find jobs in other sectors in cities and towns where at least they can be assured some money at the end of the day or month. Most villagers want to send their children to cities even though some of them admit it is too late for them to personally make the move.

India does not have a proper agricultural policy in place to give a clear vision to the future of rural India. Most policy makers and social elites have no answer as to how the rural India should be developed. The National Agricultural policy as it stands today is largely a document full of good intentions but with no practical importance. At the time of election or in emergencies like drought, the government brings fire-fighting missions that cancel electricity dues or provide greater subsidies.

The First Green Revolution created its own set of

Second Green Revolution

problems. There has been a toll on soil fertility. High Yield Value (HYVs) seeds required heavy dosages of chemicals, fertilizers and pesticides their prolonged use has depleted the soil and poisoned the environment.

Also because this form of agriculture is capital intensive, it is the rich farmer who benefits most. While India's food problems may have been solved, the hunger problem that the poor are faced with is still a prominent issue in India. Within India's society, the profits of the Green Revolution have not been spread evenly. The government had huge stocks of wheat and rice for 30 to 35 years, while the poor people were still starving because they had no income. Worst of all, in the last few years, yields are beginning to fall.

The once thrifty farmer who did not have as much water and power before the First Green Revolution, now recklessly wastes free power and water provided by the State governments. Water that accumulated for centuries has been wasted. Governments were spending huge amounts of money and tax concessions to help farmers. But few rich farmers benefited from these concessions and the majority of farmers starved -- and many committed suicide.

Instead of giving free electricity to farmers, the government should encourage loans from the banks for the use of solar and wind energy. This is a good alternative to conventional power in most areas, as there is usually plenty of sun and wind during the major part of the year. Lowering the cost of these technologies and long-term financial credit can pave the way for reducing the cost of farming. Vigorous competition among private companies in these production areas will assure the introduction of superior technologies and cost effective solutions.

Today, much of the world and India in particular, are already in water crisis and this crisis will continue to grow. Societies around the world are using more water than ever before, at increasing rates, while paying too little attention to the future consequences of that consumption. Growing populations, the depleting of ground water and the continued construction of dams on rivers will result in climate change to make this crisis all the more dire.

Water flow from Himalayan glaciers will cease in few decades

When mountains get less snow, rivers get less water and as a result, many dams on these rivers produce less clean hydroelectric power. When there is less snowmelt, farmers then need to install bigger electric pumps to get water for irrigation, and that means a greater demand for electricity from the decline of water table. Water that now flows from glaciers in the Himalayas will cease in a few decades, when those glaciers have completely melted and disappeared.

Snowmelt used to last all year long, now it stops melting in early summer; the mountain freezer is

Second Green Revolution

empty by then and snow fall starts later in the winter. Researchers say there was no question that climate change was the cause of this.

Wells are drying – falling sub-surface water table

In India people are digging millions of bore wells and pumping water out of once plentiful ground water aquifers. With an alarming rate, the water table is declining (from 100 to 150 meters below ground level and more) in almost all places. The indiscriminate use of ground water not only leads to the disappearance of resources, but also has further harmful consequences. This can lead to land subsidence - literally a collapse of the land above the aquifers. It can also lead to contamination of those aquifers with salt water, the poisoning of soil, and collapse of aquifers, that reduce their storage capacity.

In India there will be more evaporation and precipitation at higher temperatures, and storms will increase in intensity. There will be more rainfall on average, but in shorter spurts and with greater intensity. The dry land will tend to become even drier. The populous regions, with water supplies dependent on annual snowmelt and long-term glacier melt will lose water security with the disappearance of the glaciers. Water availability will decline and worsen due to rising populations, and extreme poverty and limited resources. Water shortage will worsen food security. Crop failure due to drought is likely to occur more frequently. As a result, a large number of rural households will not only lose their food supply, but their livelihood as well.

Getting more crop per drop is imperative

India needs to develop holistic plans of action for water shortage and rainfall instability. Increasing water efficiency in agriculture is needed, including the development of drought-resistant seed varieties, new irrigation strategies and increased attention to droughts through improved water storage. Increasing the productivity of agriculture without wasting water, getting more crop per drop, is necessary. What is needed is economic diversification, such as engaging 75% of rural population in non-agricultural sectors. The result should be increased employment for rural people in industry rather than in farming.

A key technological option will be to engineer crop varieties that need less water and can thrive in drought-prone areas. Such varieties can be developed either through traditional breeding techniques or through the transfer of genes from one species to another, in order to increase drought resistance. Various scientific teams are working throughout the world on crops that transfer genes from drought-resistant natural varieties to food crops, and they have achieved spectacular results in early trials.

Second Green Revolution

There is an urgent need in rural India to introduce, and in some areas increase, the use of mechanical systems to maximize the crops per drop of water. Drip irrigation is the prime example. Instead of flooding a field or bringing water to it via canals in which water can pool and evaporate, drip irrigation widely used in arid countries west of the Persian Gulf, brings a constant, low pressure stream of very small amounts of water directly to the crop roots. Water can simply be delivered through a perforated rubber hose placed on the ground near the plant's roots. This simple, affordable, and proven technology can prevent up to 90% of soil evaporation. Indian innovation of the Pepsee system should be encouraged. The Pepsee system is small plastic vials used to deliver the water, which cuts the costs of drip irrigation to very low levels.

Poor farmers in India require financial and technical help

Indian rural conditions need a low-till or no-till system for less soil evaporation. Tillers refer to the farmers' preparation of the soil for planting. Standard practices involve plowing the fields, that is, digging up the soil to remove weeds and to prepare the physical site for seeding and application of fertilizer. Low-till, or conservations tiller systems, are ways to plant the seeds with zero or minimal plowing. Thereby it accomplishes several things: soil moisture evaporation is reduced; soil structure is better maintained; and erosion is reduced. Farmers may also need special equipment to enable them to plant in untilled soil. The poor farmers in India may require financial and technical help to use special equipment.

Increasing agricultural productivity, generating rural employment and developing technology to conserve water are the challenges that need to be addressed in the development of the nation. Agricultural yield can be increased in the next few years by focusing on yield gap reduction and expanding the area of cultivation. India should do something historic: unleash reform on its vast, relatively poor, and remote or less developed part, of the country. This is where 70% of the population lives. If growth takes off here, the surrounding rural area could turn into the largest market in the world for Indian products and some foreign products.

The more sensible way for India is eco-sensitive farming. India needs to reevaluate proven, ancient ways of harmoniously maintaining soil fertility. Dependence on chemicals has to be minimized. Using quality seeds and carefully selected native breeds of plants must be encouraged if the small farmer is to be freed from unscrupulous hybrid seed companies. Indian technologies have improved considerably in the last 40 years and are available to some farmers. This was not the case in the 1960's. Technologies available in India today should be spread throughout India in all regions, especially to

Second Green Revolution

small farmers.

Most of all, agricultural pricing and market policies need to be reviewed to favor the small farmer. There are signs of an emerging awareness all around. Most significantly plant geneticist Dr M.S. Swaminathan, star of the Green Revolution is today an advocate of 'sustainable agriculture'.

A Second Green Revolution in India would take rice and wheat cultivators beyond the grain production stage, to agro-food processing and give value addition. India needs a second Green Revolution where the farmers are taken through the seed-to-grain stage involved in processing rice and value additions. The new seeds should also match the soil condition which may require less water.

The International Rice Research Institute (IRRI) in the Phillipines announced it was developing new high-yield rice hybrids to suit Indian conditions by being drought and flood-tolerant. The internationally renowned farm scientist of agriculture M S Swaminathan served as its Director General for six years in the early eighties. India is the largest financial contributor to the institute with 150,000 million dollars per year, a figure which is set to go up soon.

Several genes have been shown to confer improved drought tolerance to rice. The IRRI and its partners have identified genetic lines and hybrids that yield at least 50% more under stress than widely grown varieties such as "Swarna" and IR-36 in India.

Critics believe the problems go deeper and are rooted in India's farmers now using their land to grow "cash crops"; products such as coffee and cotton - rather than staple food crops. The input costs of cash crops are much higher than a cereal food crop, but profits are also much higher.

Now, farmers are opting for mushrooms and sweet corn; the new crops for the area. With mushrooms and baby corn, farmers get three or four crops a year, whereas with wheat and rice, they only get one crop in a season. While this economic argument may seem to be convincing, it is potentially "disastrous". India's cereal food crops are declining and hunger is on the rise.

The harvesting of mushrooms, beans, snow beans, carrots, okralla, baby corn, cotton, pepper and coffee are very profitable and popular. Farmers are now tempted to harvest more for these than staple food crops.

In India there are canals, which have brought about change in the quality of people's lives. We need many big and small canals connecting different river systems and water bodies. Most of the rivers in India are full of dirt; the cleaning and stilting of rivers is needed. India requires watersheds and rainwater management to benefit the poor people and to boost

Second Green Revolution

our agriculture and future shortages of water.

Education is most important for farmers to succeed in agricultural practices and in other fields. If three quarters (75%) of families can make sufficient money in the non-agriculture field, village life will be changed completely for the better. And with the education and knowledge farmers will be more productive with new seeds, fertilizers -- and the market with the help of computers and the internet. India needs new agricultural practices, new hybrid seeds and the establishment of cold chain and food processing units. A seed fund can be created by the government to create the right climate. Much of the other investments can be from rich farmers, banks and industries.

In the agriculture sector, India's Green Revolution of the sixties was based on research done elsewhere in the world. It was later adapted to Indian conditions. India has to find its own solution for higher yields according to their own agro-climatic conditions.

900 million people in villages cannot survive on agriculture alone

Indian agriculture will coexist in villages with manufacturing and services. Nine hundred million people in villages cannot survive on agriculture alone. In clusters of villages or in mini-new cities, the service sector will play a major part in the economy. Various forms of government services the postal services, teaching, trading, marketing, repairing, financial services including banking, real estate, human resources, media and advertising will be driven by changes in agriculture and manufacturing in rural areas. Rapid growth in rural areas will allow a greater absorption of the rural people in other activities.

Much of the routine activity, knowledge-intensive and technology-intensive conducted by the multinational and other big corporations of India will be transferred to these new cities in rural areas. As more and more people will be educated in these rural regions, cheap and educated labor will be available in these areas for IT and other industries. Indian agriculture will coexist in villages with manufacturing and services.

Many new jobs should be created in the agro-food sector. Capitalizing on the agricultural core strengths is necessary to establish a major value-adding agro-food industry based on cereals, milk, fruits, and vegetables, to generate domestic wealth. India can also be a major exporter of value added agro-food products. Agro-food industry and distribution systems should absorb large number of people rendered surplus from increasingly productive and efficient agriculture. A number of engineering industries and service businesses will grow around the agro-food sector.

Second Green Revolution: Part II

There is need to build the necessary infrastructure

required to widen the markets for India's agricultural produce. It is unsettling and painful that nearly 40% of India's harvest or crops are damaged before reaching the marketplace. Food grains are rotting in the open fields and government godowns (storage), all the while people are dying of hunger and malnutrition.

Massive Foreign Direct Investment (FDI) and private sector investment is needed to meet infrastructure needs. The US-India Business council (USIBC) has explored business opportunities in India to invest in the farm-to-market supply chain, hoping to unleash productivity and unlock the vast potential of the Indian agriculture sector. The US companies can transfer technologies and form collaborations that will make a meaningful impact on the agriculture sector.

Writer John Elliott of Fortune magazine wrote:

> "The country (India) is undergoing a second agricultural revolution--building the infrastructure that connects farm to supermarket." (August 30, 2006)

For the Second Green Revolution to succeed, private sector must play a big role in creating infrastructure: warehouses for cooling and packaging, refrigerated trucks, fleets of trucks. In India lot of crops are damaged before reaching the marketplace. There should be more storage facilities with private sector investment in infrastructure. The private sector should explore business opportunities in rural areas to invest in the farm-to-market supply chain. They can transfer technologies and form collaborations that will make a meaningful impact on the agriculture sector. Supermarket chains as announced by Mukesh Ambani of Reliance and Bharti Enterprises, Rothchild and PepsiCo are needed to meet the growing domestic demand for reliable produce.

With globalization there is a need to export to the world, using the inherent strengths of India's products. Indian farmers have learned to produce consistently high-quality crops using new seeds, fertilizers, and techniques the company provides. India has a clear cost advantage with low wages of $1 to $3 a day in a labor-intensive business.

Most small farmers lack access to non-local markets for their produce, mainly as a result of inadequate market information and transport costs. The government can assist small farmers by helping them form cooperative marketing arrangements, and by offering daily price information. The goal here should be to find ways to improve the collective bargaining power of small farmers, without the direct involvement of government officials in the determination of prices.

Ambani says he wants to deliver "better returns for the Indian farmer and producer by connecting them directly to Indian and global consumers, and lower prices and better product quality for consumers." With 70% of India's population relying on agriculture for a living, improvements in efficiency and new markets

Second Green Revolution

have the potential to benefit large numbers of people. The initiatives by Bharti, Reliance, and other companies will undoubtedly bring advantages on a large scale.

A large number of people in India, including many bureaucrats and politicians, are backing the big companies' entry into vegetables and fruits because of the obvious growth potential and the impact they can have on a farmer's performance. They are also encouraging states to relax the 'mandis' monopoly and improve infrastructure.

Leading conglomerates have pledged to overhaul the retailing sector. This will require infrastructure upgrading along the entire food distribution chain, from farm fields to store shelves.

It is hard for 900 million people to make a living with agriculture alone. Farmers and their families should have small businesses with small business loans from the banks. It is only during the harvesting and sowing season that more people should be involved in farming. Too many people are dependent on agriculture in India.

Three quarters (75%) of rural people should be employed in the non-agricultural business. Rural people should be more involved in alternative energy, computer businesses, cell phone businesses and thousands of other small (tiny) and medium businesses. These small businesses should be located in the villages where people live, or close-by small towns. This way the younger generation can be more involved with their immediate families and run tiny or small businesses closer to their villages or small towns.

As hundreds of new cities come up in the hubs of villages (in fact the whole of rural India) they will make the dream of Mahatma Gandhi come true. Simple and honest real India, "the soul of India" will become prosperous. At present pockets of very large cities, which are bulging with populations drawn largely from villages are prospering. The vastness, the variety, the vitality, the color, indeed the very pulse of India in and around villages will shine.

Summary

The food crisis is the result of increasing and growing consequences of neglect of agriculture in India. The country needs a Second Green Revolution to address the problem of food security. Over farming and a falling water table have affected the productivity that gave rise to India's Green Revolution in the mid 1960s.

India needs to develop holistic plans of action for water shortage and rainfall instability. Increasing water efficiency in agriculture is needed with new irrigation strategies and increased attention to droughts through improved water storage. Increasing the productivity of agriculture without wasting water, getting more crop per drops is necessary. In light of lack of adequate funds, small farmers are still using traditional methods of farming. Microcredit should be provided for this purpose by the banks.

The use of superior technology, such as drip irrigation, water collection, and precision application of fertilizers are required to obtain better output and higher profits. Special incentives should be provided for dry-land cultivation including the development of drought-resistant seed varieties.

Reforestation is the best method known to mankind to stop climate change. Hundreds of millions of trees should be planted throughout rural India. Wherever possible, any type of fruit tree should be planted. The Rural Employment scheme should pay for this job.

Rich farmers now recklessly waste free power and water provided by the State governments. Instead of giving free electricity to farmers, the government should encourage loans from the banks for the use of solar and wind energy, which are good alternatives to conventional power in most areas.

Much of the world and India in particular, are already in a water crisis and this crisis will continue to grow. Water that now flows from glaciers in the Himalayas will cease in a few decades, unless major changes are made and climate change is stopped or slowed down.

In India people are digging millions of bore wells and pumping water out of once plentiful ground water aquifers. With an alarming rate, the water table is declining (from 100 to 150 meters below ground level and more) in almost all places.

Most of the rivers in India are full of garbage; the cleaning and stilting of rivers is required. India needs watersheds and rainwater management to benefit the poor people, boost agriculture and avert future shortages of water.

Massive Foreign Direct Investment (FDI) and private sector investment is needed to meet infrastructure needs in India, to invest in the farm-to-market supply chain. Private sector must play a big role in creating infrastructure: a warehouses for cooling and packaging, refrigerated trucks, fleets of trucks.

In India a very large percentage of harvest in the fields or crops are damaged before reaching the marketplace. The private sector should explore business opportunities in rural areas to transfer technologies and form collaborations that will make a meaningful impact on the agriculture sector. Supermarket chains are needed to meet the growing domestic demand for reliable products.

Focus on the Poorest of the Poor

Focus on the Poorest of the Poor

In India, the worst performing states are Uttar Pradesh, Bihar and Orissa. There is a great demand for these states to reach a state of prosperity. While Goa, Delhi, Himachal Pradesh, Kerala, Haryana and Punjab, Maharashtra, Karnataka, and Gujarat perform much better and are more prosperous than the bigger states.

In the book *A View from the Outside,* P. Chidambaram, Finance Minister of India writes:

> The report (by Bibek Dubrot and Laveesh Bhandari at the India Today-organized meeting) makes out a nearly uncontestable case for small states. Goa, Delhi, Himachal Pradesh, Kerala, Haryana and Punjab easily outscore the bigger states. And among the bigger states, it is the biggest in terms of population and size that have performed the worst. With hindsight it is possible to say that the divisions of Punjab and Maharashtra were wise decisions; otherwise, would Haryana and Gujarat have recorded such impressive development? (page 222)

The consequences of unemployment, poverty, lack of education and vocational training in these states pulls down the whole country and their progress. Consider

Uttar Pradesh, Bihar and Orissa, these three states account for about 42% of all Indians living below the poverty line. They have the lowest growth rates, quality of education, lowest per capita incomes and among the poorest human development indices. According to the revised official poverty line, 37.2% of the population (about 410 million people) remain poor, making India home to one third of the world's poor people. The pace and level of urbanization has been lower in the state of Uttar Pradesh, Bihar and Orissa. Rural poverty is largely a result of low productivity and unemployment. The Indian state has undoubtedly failed in its responsibilities towards its citizens over the last 60 odd years. Poverty remains a major challenge. India cannot abandon the people of Bihar, Utter Pradesh (and Orissa) to their respective fates. The Constitution of India which lays down the fundamental right assuring its citizens justice, equality and liberty including economic freedom for all its citizens must assert itself. The Constitution that proclaims India as one nation must assert itself and these states should be provided with funds and necessary help to catch-up with the rest of India.

John F. Kennedy in his 'Inaugural address' on January 20, 1961:

> *If a free society cannot help the many who are poor, It cannot save the few who are rich.*

Great leaders of the world know that unless we uplift the poor in a democracy and free society, the elite who have gained from economic growth have reason to worry about its trends. The rich society in India should not feel very secure because they are doing very well. The rich should be worried about the poor, as their progress is very slow. Indians should be concerned about unemployment, water shortage and climate change in the country. India cannot abandon the poor states and especially the rural poor people.

India must help the poorer districts on war footing

The central government must act to provide infrastructure, jobs, bank loans, and industries for Uttar Pradesh, Bihar and Orissa on war footing. Dividing the states of Uttar Pradesh and Bihar into smaller states is a very controversial subject and has lots of problems attached to it. A better alternative may be that the central government directly assists the poorer districts of these states. This should be done on war footing before a catastrophe hits these states, such as running out of water (in the light of falling water tables in the next five years).

Additionally, the fear that the Himalayan glaciers will meltdown in the major parts of these states in a couple of decades is of grave concern. With global warming, water shortages are already felt throughout India. If improvements and changes are not made now, there will be a disaster in these states soon. India will have a population of 1.5 billion people by

2025. It will become more and more difficult to manage these states as the population continues to multiply.

Central government should fund and appoint an administrator

India should have Centrally Administered District Administration (CADA) in the very poorest districts of these large and other poor states. These districts should be run by an administrator appointed and funded by the central government and directly under the control of the Prime Minister. The administrator would be responsible for the delivery of selected public goods until they are self- sufficient and prosperous. The result will be approximately 50 units of CADA administered areas. The administrator's responsibility would be to provide people with jobs and bank loans for existing mini and small businesses and new startups. Another responsibility of the administrator would be to improve education, vocational training, health care, water supply, electricity, road and sanitation in his district. The mind-set of the central government should be very important. No state government should feel that it is a punishment for some of their wrong doing. In fact these backward states and especially the rural poor districts have done very poorly under any party rule, both before independence and since then.

Some essential requirements for the administrator

Some common requirements for the administrator of the district working directly under the Prime Minister are as follows. First, the man or woman who heads the project must be given a tenure of say five to ten years. Second, these districts must be given the funds required, not on an annual basis, but on project-cost improvement basis, with the power to draw and spend. Third, in these special districts the decision-making process should come directly from the administrator downward, like in the private sector. Decisions should travel from the top to the bottom. In the private sector, an executive director ensures that a decision is taken by a board of directors, is passed-on and communicated downward for implementation. It should be noted that this is the way decisions are implemented in China -- and is the reason for their tremendous success. The usual decision-making process with the government of India and the states is from the bottom to top, as was started under British rule.

Fourth, it is the administrator's responsibility to make quick decisions. There is a tendency among civil servants to avoid taking sides to reach a decision on a financial or controversial matter. This fear of taking a side is a major cause of delay in the decision making process. Finally, the administration should have greater authority and accountability. The head of the project must be held accountable for good or bad results. A system of punishment and rewards would encourage these officials to take proper action.

Talented young men or women will be appointed to fill in the positions of an administrator and other officials in these poor districts. They would be given five to ten years of contract, with the mandate to conceive, plan, implement and show success. They should be assured resources, freedom of action, with no interference in the discharge of their duties. Bureaucratic and interference of the politicians must be completely eliminated in these districts for at least ten years or until these districts are prosperous. It is essential to follow a rule-based system of administration, which circumscribes the powers of politicians and confers greater authority on the civil service itself for self-regulations. With empowerment comes great accountability; the civil servants must be up to par in terms of performance and ethical conduct.

Suggestions and ideas for the Administrator to overhaul the poor districts

The administrator should start a drastic overhaul of the existing poor districts. Education and employment should be the top priority. Education is most important for farmers to succeed in agricultural practices and in other fields. If three quarters (75%) of these families can make money in the non-agriculture field, village life will be changed completely for the better. With vision and acumen, the administrator will start the change and with economic progress in these districts, every part of this great country could become prosperous. It should be made clear that politicians will have no part to play in day-to-day administration of these districts for ten years.

National Rural Employment Guarantee Act (NREGA) should be provided to the parents of the school children, where required. The idea is to provide employment to poor, unemployed and marginal farmers and farm workers. The result will be reduced dropout rates for rural children once there is some kind of stability for parents by way of an employment guarantee scheme. Economic reasons are number one for dropout rates in schools. The Government should also give financial help in the form of scholarships or stipends to children of poor families. This could be in the form private tuition by senior students.

Rural unemployment scheme for substitute teachers

A number of teachers are absent in schools on any given day in rural India. And on the other hand there are many educated unemployed people in the villages. If they can get any type of job locally, they would choose to stay in their own villages. Here some type of rural employment scheme is needed for educated people to work as substitute teachers or teacher helpers. Teacher helpers, with some training in education should be utilized. Almost all parents of these school children are uneducated and cannot help their children with their homework. This is why the role of the teacher helper is so important.

The administrator should overhaul the education system. The education system should be job oriented and vocational training should be a major part of it. Reducing dropout rates should be the government's major responsibility. Administrators should make sure that the studies are interesting enough for children. Physical punishment of students by teachers (and abusive language by teachers) should be completely eliminated. Ragging by senior students should be banned. Administrators should make sure that at any given time there are sufficient teachers or teacher helpers teaching in the school. The number of teachers must be increased considerably for students to receive an adequate quality of education.

The poor people who live in these districts have been discriminated against throughout their lives. Whether intentional or not, this population at a major financial disadvantage have been ignored completely. Even small skills are not taught to these people. Some families had a monopoly, and these skills were passed down to only a small percentage of youths. What India needs in these poor districts is some vocational training in all the Primary and Secondary schools as part of their syllabus.

India requires vocational training programs to prepare

the youth for a vocation of their choice. India should build up a large trained workforce. In the manufacturing and service sectors there are hundreds of skills and vocations for which there is a worldwide shortage. For example: TV, electrical appliance repair and service, automobile repair and service, medical and health services, nursing and other paramedics. India requires millions of trained people in the area of services for agriculture, floriculture, horticulture, fisheries, healthcare, tourism and hundreds of skills for the manufacturing sector. By supplying world class skilled people required by the nation and for rest of the world, India will reduce its unemployment. The country must be run with higher efficiency, less wastage and lower costs of operation. This can be accomplished by providing vocational training.

In India 900 million people live in rural areas. Most of them are dependent on agriculture for their livelihood. Every few years the monsoon fails and agriculture does not provide income for the poor. Capital investment in the agriculture sector should compensate or increase for the inadequate monsoon. Public investment in agriculture as a percentage of GDP should increase. The story of employment is equally dismal. Another way to put more money in the hands of the poor is to ensure that they receive jobs in the industrial sector in mini-new cities in the hubs of villages.

India can have prices as low as China's

If rural people in education and vocational sectors are taught and trained, India can have prices as low as China's prices. Even Grade 5 drop-outs in rural areas can be given vocational training. These youths can be involved in manufacturing. This is the only way to begin to catch up with China in the field of manufacturing. Indian companies should be given incentives to start new factories in these rural areas. New cities in the hubs of villages and Special Economic Zones (SEZ) should be developed in the heart of village clusters.

The National Rural Employment Guarantee Act (NREGA), of which India is very proud of, pays for 100 days of work at minimum wages. This is very beneficial for people who work or make sufficient income to support themselves and their families. If this scheme gives 300 days of work opportunity, Indian workers in rural areas will be very happy and they can use this money to support their families better. With the low cost of living in the rural areas and so much unemployment or underemployment, a very large number of factories should be attracted to them. The wages in these rural areas will be very competitive, as compared to Chinese wages and will attract thousands of Indian and foreign companies to these locations.

The Chinese model of development is based on providing employment through infrastructure development in various smaller towns and Special Economic Zones (SEZ). These models of rural business hubs add value to agricultural produce within the rural area. The Chinese take a holistic view of rural development in which all the activities are integrated to have optimal use of their resources.

China has so many low-wage workers at the unskilled, semiskilled, and skilled level, because it has such a large industrial base including factory, equipment, and knowledge jobs to keep its workers employed. Young workers and managers are willing to work twelve-hour days. They have an entrepreneurial spirit to do whatever it takes to please big international retailers such as Wal-Mart, Best Buy, J C Penney and Target stores.

With the improvement of conditions, these very poor districts during the next five to ten years, India will be transformed into a developed country. There is a saying that the strength of a chain is judged by its weakest link. It is also true that the strength or weakness of the country is judged by its number of poor and starving people. This improvement would be achieved within the framework of democracy, with full backing from the people. By 2018-2020, India would reach its goal of becoming a developed country.

For the most part, manufacturing growth in India is dependent on agricultural growth. When agricultural growth declines, manufacturing growth declines with it. The manufacturing sector should not be allowed to be dragged down by the decline in the agriculture sector. The effect of poor agricultural production cannot be entirely avoided, especially with the current state of global warming and climate change. Corrective measures can be taken to maintain the momentum of the manufacturing sector. India needs insurance that interest rates will remain low. There is increase in public investment and private investment is encouraged, both from domestic and foreign sources. This calls for close monitoring and attention to detail within these projects and that the backward district Administrator ensures the projects are started and completed on schedule.

A Second Green Revolution is needed to bridge the rural-urban divide and help advance India into a developed nation. Agriculture cannot afford to be brought down; India's economy depends on agriculture as its largest employer. A Second Green Revolution is necessary in light of the agricultural growth rate that has plummeted in the last few years. This is in spite of the fact that India has a competitive advantage in agriculture, with plenty of arable land, sunshine, and water.

There is urgent need in rural India to introduce, and in some areas increase the use of mechanical systems to maximize the crops per drop of water. Drip irrigation is the prime example. Drip irrigation should be used instead of flooding a field or bringing water to it via canals in which water can pool and evaporate. Drip irrigation brings a constant, low pressure stream of very small amounts of water directly to the crop roots. Water can simply be delivered through a perforated rubber hose and placed on the ground near the plant's roots. This method is simple, affordable, and its proven technology can prevent up to 90% of soil evaporation. India has also made innovations to the irrigation systems, including the Pepsee system of drip irrigation. This irrigation system of using small plastic vials should be encouraged.

Education is most important for farmers to succeed in agricultural practices and in other fields. If three quarters (75%) of these families can make money in the non-agricultural fields, village life will be entirely changed for the better. With the necessary education and knowledge, farmers will be able to do better with new seeds, fertilizers and the market, with the help of the computer and internet. India needs new agricultural practices, new hybrid seeds and the establishment of cold chain and food processing units. A seed fund can be created by the government to create the right climate. Other investments can come from wealthy farmers, banks and industries.

Many new jobs could be created in the agro-food sector. India must capitalize on the agricultural core strengths to establish a major value-adding agro-food industry based on cereals, milk, fruits, and vegetables, to generate domestic wealth. Also, making India a major exporter of value added agro-food products will ensure huge benefits. Agro-food industry and distribution systems will absorb a number of people rendered surplus from increasingly productive and efficient agriculture.

A number of engineering industries and service businesses will grow around the agro-food sector. India has a clear cost advantage with low wages of $1 to $3 a day in a labor-intensive business.

Since urban areas are centers of industrial and business activities in light of economies of scale, more and more new towns should be established or seeded in the midst of the rural hubs. Wealth begets wealth. Higher economic activity stimulates more economic activities and therefore more employment. Most big cities are becoming unlivable, about 50% of their inhabitants live in slums or near slum conditions. A number of studies have shown that if a city becomes too big, it becomes much more costly to provide services to the increasing population in a city than it would to establish a new city. There are some estimates how much it costs the government per person in a big city. The cost is roughly 10 times more to the governments (free electricity and water and other benefits for slums) than it would cost them in small cities in the hubs of the villages. These are estimates, as no official study has been done.

India should build hundreds of new towns and base the economy of the town on a combination of fields including: manufacturing, service and agriculture. The basic model is simple. Let's say a developer acquires a sufficiently large piece of non-prime, inexpensive land. The developer could be a public-private consortium who makes improvements, such as adding utility, roads and buildings. Then he proceeds to get a few big commercial interests and anchor tenants to locate themselves on this land and sell or rent subdivisions to whoever wants it. Improvements to the land would begin would begin and as the work proceeds stage by stage, small bits are sold off to interested parties to pay for these on-going improvements.

The anchor firms will expand their output. This is in light of anticipation that the economy will grow rapidly as new cities are being built. The demand for labor will go up. Labor will come primarily from the agriculture sector and will be highly productive in non-agriculture sectors such as services and manufacturing. Even though the economy of the regions will grow at a very fast rate, there will be no inflation.

All sorts of service providers will move in or come in to the area, from schools to shopping, banks to bakeries. With sufficient income for the workers who will purchase the agricultural and manufacturing products and service units, there will be all around growth. Employed workers will use their income to buy food and housing, which will become affordable.

Half of government's budget should go to 70% of the poor

Half of the cenaltral and state government's budgets should be diverted to programs designed to bring sustained benefits to the poorest 70% of the population, especially in rural areas. A quarter of the budget should be focused on physical infrastructure, particularly in the backward districts. International funds and local funds should be encouraged to support Indian infrastructure. Money should be available to meet all genuine development needs. International funds are not coming to these backward districts, where the poor are the poorest people in the world. International agencies believe that India no longer qualifies for these funds. This is because India has lots of foreign reserves and it is believed that India can take care of these poor people. This is against the trend in African and other poor Asian countries where they feel outside help is necessary.

The key to jobs is investment. China has invested massive amounts of capital investment in core areas such as power, telecommunications, roads and railways. India on the other hand has not invested anywhere near as much capital. A massive amount of capital investment is needed in core areas, especially in the backward districts.

Corruption has an adverse effect on growth, development and poverty reduction. Research has established that corruption reduces productivity, lowers investment, causes fiscal drain and has a devastating effect on efficiency. In India, programs seldom yield the kind of positive economic results that are initially expected. Corruption has a significant negative impact on the rate of return on projects. The relationship between corruption and investment explain the 'poverty trap' in which India finds itself. The effect of corruption is more felt by small enterprises and the overall growth of employment in the economy. For small industries, it raises costs and reduces profits because they have to make payments that do not contribute to productivity or output, but are necessary for their survival.

In the book *The Future of India*, Bimal Jalan writes:

> Since independence, in addition to giving various incentives to promote small enterprises, central and state governments have launched a variety of anti-poverty rural development and special employment programmes to directly benefit the poor and the disadvantaged. Most of the benefits of these programmes are also appropriated by bureaucrats and middlemen at various levels of the administrative hierarchy. Thus, in a memorable and widely quoted observation, after visiting some of these programmes Prime Minister Rajiv Gandhi had pointed out that 'out of Rs. 100 crores allocated to an anti-poverty project, I know that only Rs. 15 crores reaches the people. The remainder is gobbled up by middlemen, power brokers, contractors and the corrupt'. (page 123).

Government has not spent money allotted for specific purposes

There are many reasons why progress has not been made in the poorest districts of UP, Bihar and Orissa. One of the most important is that the central and state governments have not spent the amount set apart or allotted for the agricultural and allied sector. While the funds were promised, details of the projects such as where the money is needed and where it can actually be spent during the fiscal year have not been worked out. Even if the details were worked out, most of the time the officers in charge would be transferred so frequently that no one took on the responsibility of seeing the projects completed. Moreover, these plans or schemes are to be implemented by the state governments, where the quality of governance is so poor that the schemes simply run over from year to year without being completed and without yielding results. For this reason central governments should take on this responsibility of uplifting hundreds of millions of people, especially in the poorest districts of poor states.

In India 70% of the total workforce is engaged or employed in the agricultural sector and allied fields. The population is very large and incomes are very small in these rural areas. The result is that most of these areas have very low per capita income; India as a whole has very low per capita income. In the absence of the industrial and service sector in these rural regions, the dependence of 70% is mostly on agriculture. The low level of agricultural income is attributed to low prices of produce; a price barely adequate to cover the farmer's cost of producing. Most of the benefits that the government gives to these rural people are gobbled up by rich farmers, politicians, bureaucrats and middle men. In addition to free electricity, free water and many other incentives and benefits which the government gives, the majority of these benefits are taken by a small number of rich farmers. They do not pay any income tax on their income, which in turn could have gone to the poor and unemployed farmers.

Additional suggestion and ideas for the Administrator

Technology serves as the highest generator of wealth in the shortest period of time. Technology reaches multiple areas such as education and training, agriculture and food processing, industries and infrastructure in various fields. Electric power is the most important part of the infrastructure. India already has the technology to dramatically change its current rural, social and economic conditions. There is an abundance of sunshine, where solar energy can be produced in abundance. The growth of a nation's GDP is vitally linked to the availability of electric power.

The backward district administrators should invite private industries in their areas. Some of the private sector industries have quality training programs to upgrade their personnel. The contribution of this sector has been recognized not only in the consumer sector, but also in infrastructure and strategic industries.

The administrators should urge both big and medium-sized industries to their districts to add at least one project on their own, in addition to their business operations at other locations in India. These industries will see a lot of future business and growing profits.

The administrator should invite Small Industries (SI) units to their areas. Small industries contribute to more than 40% of Indian industrial output. Some units from bigger cities would love to move to these districts because of many advantages, including: larger, less expensive land and an abundance of cheap labor. These districts should encourage existing units from bigger cities and new units to be established in the region.

Some new cities should be seeded in these poor districts. There is plenty of land, labor and raw material available in these areas. In the past the mass production was only confined to a few locations. With modern technology, it is possible to have a number of decentralized industries in these rural districts. These industries would maintain world-class levels and become part of a globally competitive industry. Electricity, especially solar and wind energy can be supplied anywhere. The vital modern telecommunication and IT infrastructure has made global connectivity instantaneous.

It is possible to connect clusters of villages into a new town or city and in doing so, India would see great benefits. Many agro industries, service industries and even high tech concerns can be relocated in such new cities by moving a few government offices and providing special concessions for industries. India must capitalize on the agricultural core strengths to establish a major value-adding agro-food industry based on cereals, milk, fruits and vegetables in order to generate local wealth in these rural districts. Once the process of value-adding agro-food industry starts, economic activities will generate in a big way.

Industry and trade is the best guarantee of development and prosperity. Industry and trade drive the world's economy as well as a nation's economy. The more a country trades and has industries in hubs of villages or mini-new cities close to villages, the more prosperous it will become.

The central government must promote investment in regions where the potential for job creation is the highest. It should encourage labor intensive industries in new cities in the hubs of rural areas or Special Economic Zones (SEZ). Public and private investment is required in areas with roads, irrigation works, solar power, tourism, textile industry, and railways. Railways and advanced textile industries, and other key industries should be expanded and modernized, (as loans from the bank will be very easily available to railways to expand and modernize).

Although cities are important, Indian economic policies must not ignore villages. As long as 70% of Indians live in rural areas and the workforce is dependent on agriculture, Indian economic policies must be directed towards their welfare. It should be noted that no country has achieved growth and prosperity through a village-based model of development. This is why India requires mini-new cities in the middle of these villages or hubs of villages. China, which in many ways resembles India, abandoned the village-based model of development long ago and developed hundreds of new towns and cities. Tens of thousands of industries were built in the hubs of villages or in new cities and hundreds of millions of jobs were generated for the unemployed and under employed.

In China the manufacturing sector, especially in new cities, has absorbed hundreds of millions of people coming out of rural areas. In India this economy of scale will work in new cities as well. Labor class and lower middle class people can afford to buy houses in these new cities. India has about 70%, or 900 million people spread over 600,000 villages. Clearly there is no need to urbanize all the villages, however new cities in the hubs of the villages is the best alternative. It is not necessary for people to migrate to the existing mega cities, which are already bursting at the seams. In most big cities the conditions are becoming unlivable as a very large number of their inhabitants live in slums or near slum conditions. Beyond the factor of lack of space, it becomes much more costly to provide services to the increasing population in a big city than to establish a new city in the hubs of the village groupings.

Banks are flushed with money and this money should be channeled into business and agriculture in the rural areas. Agriculture and small businesses need micro loans from the banks and other sources. Even big businesses in these areas will need large bank loans.

India should have a job creation policy for the less educated and uneducated young men and women in rural areas. The unemployed workforce lives largely in rural areas. In despair they migrate to the cities, adding to the woes of urban areas. India needs to implement massive irrigation and road-building projects. To this can be added textile, shoes, and other leather products. Improvements to railways should be made, including in rural areas. Railways should lay more rail lines in these poor districts. The capital investment of railways must be enhanced. Every irrigation project must be given funds to be completed in double-quick time.

Schools, water, roads, electricity and sanitation are basic needs in a civilized society. Public and government institutions have failed to deliver these public goods. From a health care perspective, the first budget in 2008 has given some focus and incentive to the private sector. In fact, according to some estimates, India needs a huge amount of investment for basic health care. India's rank is at a poor 112 (as per WHO country rankings), far behind in terms of infrastructure: beds, doctors and nurses. More hospitals are required in the hubs of rural areas or new cities, so that villagers do not have to travel to big cities for medical attention and treatment.

India should create rural business hubs using the

Chinese model. China managed to achieve in a dozen years what it took the Western world a century to accomplish. India should also follow China's example in attracting foreign capital, industry and disciplined ways of doing things. China has achieved success, because they do things in a very big way and on war footing, without any red tape or bureaucracy. Its economic output will grow to $4 trillion (U.S.) by 2020, from 1.6 trillion today and its output per capita, a more accurate measure of wealth, will triple to $3,000 per person.

China has avoided the Indian based model of development because that would slow their country's progress; they are learning from India what not to do. The Chinese want to show their best cities and their best side to the world. Their show resembles business people who go to the market or banks to borrow money and do whatever it takes to please big retailers to obtain business. In India many investors are turned off with India's poor infrastructure, poverty and slums in urban areas, labor laws and lax way of doing things.

If India wants to benefit from the flattening of the world and interconnecting of the market and knowledge centres, it will have to try to keep up with China. There are some success stories already in India, and these need to be emulated, built on and expanded across many sectors. The manufacturing sector has to be one of the biggest drivers for growth. Over the coming years, this sector needs to absorb the tens of millions of people coming out of rural India. The manufacturing sector and service sector will go hand in hand.

Summary

The central government must directly assist the poorest districts of poor states like Uttar Pradesh, Bihar and Orissa to provide infrastructure, jobs, bank loans, and industries. This should be done on war footing before a catastrophe hits these states.

The most backward districts should be run by an administrator appointed and funded by the central government, directly under the control of the Prime Minister.

The administrator would be responsible for the delivery of selected public goods until they are self-sufficient and prosperous. This would provide people with jobs, owning small businesses, provision of water, road and sanitation.

Some common requirements for the administrator of such districts are as follows:

1. The man or woman who heads the project must be given a tenure of five to ten years, for continuity in implementation.
2. These districts must be given the funds required, not on an annual basis, but on a project-cost improvement basis, with the power to draw and spend.

3. In these special districts, the decision-making process should come directly from the administrator downward, like in the private sector. Decisions should travel from the top to the bottom.
4. It is the administrator's responsibility to make quick decisions. There is a tendency among civil servants to avoid taking a side to reach a decision on a financial or controversial matter. This fear of making a decision is a major cause of delay in the decision making process.
5. The administration should have greater authority and accountability. The head of the project must be held accountable for good or bad results. A system of punishment and rewards would encourage these officials to take proper action.

Talented young men or women will be appointed to fill in the positions of an administrator and other officials in these poor districts. They would be given five to ten years of contract, with the mandate to conceive, plan, implement and show success.

The Administrators should be assured of resources, freedom of action, with no interference in the discharge of their duties. Bureaucracy and interference of politicians will be completely eliminated in these districts for at least ten years or until these districts are prosperous.

The administrators should start a drastic overhaul of the

existing poor districts. Education and employment should be the top priority.

With vision and acumen, the administrators will start the change and with economic progress in these districts, every part of this great country could become prosperous.

The administrators should invite public and private sector industries in their areas. They should invite Small Industries (SI) units to their areas.

The administrators should get both big and medium-sized industries to their districts to add at least one project in the district, in addition to their business operations at other locations in India.

Some new towns with infrastructure to grow into cities, should be seeded in these poor districts. With modern technology, it is possible to have a number of decentralized industries in these rural districts regions.

Electricity, especially solar and wind energy can be supplied anywhere. The vital modern telecommunication and IT infrastructure has made global connectivity instantaneous.

India Calling

India is the world's largest democracy and the 4th largest economy in terms of purchasing power parity. With its consistent growth performance and highly-skilled manpower, India provides enormous opportunities for investment in various sectors. With the rapidly changing global economy, it is becoming clear that North America and Europe need to diversify their economic relationship with India. These countries now recognize that India will be one of the leading growth engines of the 21st century world economy.

India's institutions guarantee security of long-term investments

A series of ambitious economic reforms aimed at deregulating the economy and stimulating foreign investment has moved India firmly into the league of front-runners of the rapidly growing Asian Pacific region countries and unleashed the latent strength of a complex and rapidly changing nation. Today, India is one of the most exciting emerging markets in the world. Skilled managerial and technical manpower that matches the best available in the world and an emerging middle class, provides India with a distinct cutting edge in global competition. India's time tested institutions offer foreign investors a transparent environment that guarantees the security of their long-term investment. This includes a free and vibrant press, a well-establish judiciary, a sophisticated legal and accounting system and a user- friendly intellectual infrastructure. India's dynamic and highly competitive industrial sector has long been the backbone of its economic activity and offers considerable scope for foreign direct investment, joint venture and collaborations.

India's (economic) performance is now second only to China's, and the world has taken notice. The country has improved its foreign exchange position considerably. Now foreign exchange reserves are almost US$ 320 billion. India is now an effective net creditor to the rest of the world. China's export is still considerably much more; their imports plus exports is 75% of their economy, which is considerably larger than that of India.

India is the latest of a series of Asian countries that have been transformed by economic development in the last two decades. The East Asian growth model consists of an export-oriented strategy that uses heavy investment in manufacturing capacity and infrastructure to drive development. These economies usually started out with low-skill exports like making ready-made garments, toys and cheap household items. Now the exports include things like high-end electronics and automobiles, and the infrastructure has improved considerably.

India fast emerging as one of most favored investment destinations

India is fast emerging as one of the most favored investment destinations in the world. A number of studies and surveys in the recent past have highlighted the growing attractiveness of India as an investment destination. During 2008-2009, India received foreign direct investment (FDI) worth US$ 27.31 billion. Investment (FDI) worth US $20.92 billion flowed into the country during April-December 2009. Investor sentiment is very positive and the investment (FDI) looks set to cross US$ 25 billion in India during 2009-10.

India's foreign policy has been formulated with a view to inviting and encouraging investment into India. The process of regulation and approval has been substantially liberalized. Investment under automatic route is permitted in most activities, except a few where prior approval of the government is required. Foreign direct investment into India has risen at an annual rate pace of 21 % over the past decade, and corporate India is emerging as a dominant outward investor. The $75 billion of overseas investment during the past decade reflects the rising trend of Indian companies seeking a North America presence. India is seeking that presence to leverage its lower cost home production base as well as to enhance its technological capabilities and expand supply chain relationships.

The Government of India welcomes foreign direct investment (FDI)

The Government of India welcomes investment (FDI), especially for development of infrastructure, technological up-gradation of Indian industry through investment and in projects having the potential of creating employment opportunities on a large scale. Investment for setting up Special Economic Zones (SEZs) and establishing manufacturing units, are also welcomed. India is one of the most attractive investment destinations across the globe due to its rapidly rising per capita income; surging manufacturing sector; expanding high technology and service sectors; renewed focus on infrastructure and natural resources requirements; and its accelerated pace of market deregulation.

East Asians are now interested in establishing factories in India. The Government of India welcomes the investment (FDI) from these East Asian countries. The key difference with the East Asian model is that India did not see a major acceleration in investment activity until after 2000. As pointed out by numerous studies, heavy investment is a key driver of the usual East Asian model. The most extreme of the East Asian model is China, with an investment rate of around 48% of GDP.

Large scope for manufacturing industries in India

The most dramatic difference with East Asia was the sector that generated growth. In East Asia, export oriented manufacturing and construction was the boom sector. In contrast, the service sector in India has generated the bulk of the growth. This means that there is large scope for manufacturing industries in India. The scope is as large in India as it was 20 to 25 years ago in China. In next 5 to 10 years India will have very high domestic saving rates. It is easier for multinational manufacturing companies to enter India now with investment (FDI) than later.

India is going through the same East Asia miracle, which caused growth from Japan, to Korea and Taiwan, and then to China. China's recent performance may be dramatic due to its sheer scale and speed but it is merely the latest manifestation of the standard East Asian model. In India, there are millions of people who aspire to lift themselves out of poverty. On the other hand there are vast opportunities, which remain unexplored. India is in a process of uplifting the rural masses and providing jobs to them. India is serious about attracting a much higher level of Foreign Direct Investment from multinational manufacturing companies and expatriate Indians planning their return home.

The growth process took several centuries in the West and a few decades in Asia. In fact, Europe also went through a process that parallels the East Asian experience, although this was spread over centuries.

The difference is that Asia went through this shift within a very concentrated time span of a few decades. The rising importance of India in world economy is more than visible.

India needs labour intensive industries

There is nothing wrong with debt for development. Loans used prudently are the heartbeats of a modern economy. There is no doubt that labor intensive growth can deliver very rapid advancement to an underdeveloped economy and upgrade standards of living at an unprecedented pace. These factors allow for large productivity gains for the host country as new infrastructure is put in place and new technologies are imported. In other words, there is nothing wrong with a developing country that generates growth by using investment and literacy, to absorb technologies that already exist in the rest of the world.

More than half of the Fortune 500 companies have some 'presence' in India. It is these companies which control capital, technology, brands and markets. These multinational and other foreign companies can provide huge capital, provided India can negotiate with them on the highest level of government. Targeting the Fortune 500 companies, plus thousands of other foreign companies is an excellent strategy. It is also to the advantage of these companies to start manufacturing in India, in addition to other places. It is best to have a presence in dissimilar markets to spread the risk. India is a democracy and will always remain so and the rule of law prevails in the country. India is a land of opportunity for a foreign investor.

The information revolution has accelerated the rise of the global economy. We are living in a time that will be remembered and studied for generations. The size of the global economy has doubled every ten years or so, going from $31 trillion in 1999 to $62 trillion in 2008. Over the past few decades, countries all over the world have been experiencing rates of economic growth that were once unthinkable. This growth has been most visible in Asia, but is no longer confined to these areas.

Multinational corporations are moving globally

Multinational Corporations and capital are moving from place to place, finding the best location in which to do business. The emerging global system is likely to be quite different from those that have preceded it. Most of the developed world has become conscious of the changing world. Multinational businesses are increasingly aware of the shifts taking place around the world and responding to them rapidly and unemotionally. Large US based multinationals almost uniformly report that their growth now relies on penetrating new foreign markets. With annual revenue growth of 2-3% a year in the United States, and 10-15% a year abroad, they know they have to adapt to new globalized world – or else lose out.

India has an open door policy now. India should do things at an accelerated pace and assure foreign private enterprise one window and open window policy. The Indian Government should extend a welcome mat to foreign investors. Multinational should have greater choices in India. Indian central government, the States and municipalities should have one window policy and should encourage more multinational manufacturing investment. India should also encourage and rely on Indian expatriates to provide capital. The welcoming of the overseas Indian (diaspora) will pay many dividends. These policies will bring India lots of jobs and make India a prosperous country.

India should view expatriates as part of the national fabric.

India can learn a lot from China about expatriate (diaspora) management: economic incentives coupled with patriotic sentiments – for the country's economic advantage. By consistently welcoming its diaspora, India can take its economy forward. India should view the expatriate (diaspora) as part of the national fabric, a source to stimulate the country's economic development and modernization. A very large percentage of foreign direct investment can be brought in by this group. The wealth and investment, and Indian relationship will be mutually beneficial. Indian diaspora could provide a wealth of ideas, followed by financing on a large scale.

In the late 1970s, 1980s and 1990s, North American immigrants from India were mostly doctors, engineers, academics, and entrepreneurs. These highly skilled professionals achieved such visibility and prominence in North American host countries that even India, initially reluctant, was forced to recognize them. This group of engineers and entrepreneurs brought the diaspora to everyone's attention.

India should establish an Overseas Indian Affairs office in every State, region and in many municipalities, with the goal of systematically building a relationship with the diaspora. Through the 1980s, China was setting up organizations to cater to the needs of overseas Chinese. India should also invite successful, emotionally connected groups of individuals who are willing to give back to their country of origin. The government's first concrete action to attract NRI investment was to float the Resurgent India Bonds in July 1998 by the State Bank of India, which was very successful.

In China success did not come overnight. It resulted from a series of systemic and organized experiments. FDI was first tested in four Special Economic Zones in Guangdong and Fujian provinces, where the Chinese created conditions that would be conducive to investment. In the second phase of the experiment, the Chinese opened fourteen more cities across ten provinces to FDI. From 1984 to 1988 FDI inflow averaged just over $2 billion annually. In 1992 Deng Xiaoping's promised and committed China to economic reforms, FDI inflow surged the next year from $4 billion to $11 billion. Ups and downs followed, although FDI reached $44 billion in 1992. In 2001 China concluded its decade-long negotiations to enter the World Trade Organization (WTO).

In China, Deng established a framework and gave local governments incentive to pursue foreign investment (FDI). The Chinese gave foreign investors red carpet treatment. Local party officials were rewarded for attracting foreign investment. In India, the central government should give the States incentive to help attract foreign investors.

India is unconnected to multinational corporations

Initially Microsoft faced daunting challenges in China for at least 10 years. Now their relations are very cooperative and friendly. On April 18, 2006, President HU Jintao arrived in the United States. His first stop was not Washington, D.C. but Redmond, Washington, home to Microsoft Corporation, and its founder Bill Gates. At Microsoft's headquarters, Hu exclaimed, "Because you, Mr. Bill Gates, are a friend of China, I'm a friend of Microsoft. It was a shining moment in the decade-long Microsoft- China relations that had its share of dark days.

Ultimately Microsoft's strategy in China focuses on long-term investment. They now cooperate with local Chinese industry, partners and government organizations to build up a win-win relationship and to help China embrace the knowledge economy. Microsoft is aware of the Chinese government's policy to boost local software industry. Microsoft announced that they would explore opportunities to establish joint venture with the government and local companies.

The Chinese Government often goes out of its way to offer numerous concessions to attract potential customers and multinational manufacturing industries. China favors multinational companies who are working exclusively for China, and give them direct support. For example, if Unilever has deep roots in India, China would develop its global rival, Proctor & Gamble for China. Once they start business with a company they keep them very busy in China, and also develop other products. Motorola was a Western pioneer in China and has grown into a great success story. Meanwhile, India is unconnected to these operations.

The building of the Motorola manufacturing plant in Tianjin began in July 1992, and up until 2003 the company invested $3.4 billion in manufacturing and research and development facilities, more than any other Western company. As the Chinese operations became more important, a hotline of sort was established between Beijing and the company's headquarters in Schaumburg, Illinois. Meanwhile the Motorola operations in India had to first report to Singapore and then navigate a long bureaucratic trail before reaching Schaumburg. It is easy to see why the company's familiarity with India developed more slowly and ultimately was far less than its familiarity with China, where the company was assured direct support from the Chinese Government.

There is a need for the Indian Prime Minister to be in touch with the multinationals investing or intending to bring Foreign Direct Investment (FDI) in India. Also, to give confidence to the multinational, there should be a high level committee of Deputy Prime Minister (India does not have one at present) or a very senior minister and the leader of the opposition. There is a protocol that when a foreign head of the state visits another country (India), they meet the leader of the opposition in addition to the Prime Minister and the President. Similarly, the leader of the opposition should be in touch with the foreign companies. This is the best way to build confidence.

Full weight of Prime Minister's authority

The Prime Minister along with the ruling party president are very powerful. Many people blame democracy for delays and give the credit to China for its "fait accompli" authority for rapid progress. But, whatever and whenever the government of India wants to do something, they get it done. The need of the hour is for the Prime Minister to initiate progress faster for the rural masses. All this can be done under democracy. The leader can only be the Prime Minister and cannot be central government ministers, chief ministers of states or bureaucrats. They can all be extension of his power but can only act as his arms, with the exception of some cases involving the Chief Minister of states. Many chief ministers proved to be very successful in their states.

Mr. P. Chidambaram is the Home Minister in the present central government. He had been Finance Minister also with the central government. In the book written by P. Chidambaram, 'A View from the Outside':

> The case for FDI (foreign direct Investment) is too well known. FDI brings in additional investible resources, modern technologies, access to markets and better and more efficient management practices. Wise countries encourage their people to save; wiser countries entice those savings to their lands by providing opportunities for investment. (page 39)
>
> We need both domestic savings and the savings of the people of other countries. These savings are investible resources. Developing nations like India are in dire need of such resources. (page 39)

No Prime Minister has put the full weight of his authority behind a drive to attract more FDI. (page 40)

The Central Government has all the money and are all-powerful in initiating policies. Unlike China, Indian states continue to be heavily dependent on central grants for carrying various schemes and programs of rural development. Most states now cannot fiscally undertake even minimal essential investment or maintenance expenditure. The need of the hour is to freeze the salary of the central and state government employees for 5 years. This is because people in rural areas are making a mere fraction of the money that organized sector employees make.

FDI euphoria is far greater in China than in India

The FDI euphoria is far greater in China than in India. The multinationals in China create a lot of value by providing goods and services, Chinese consumers wish to buy. Or multinationals make things more cheaply for their customers outside China.

The payment might take many forms or it is likely to be direct. The Chinese provincial governments often go out of their way to offer numerous concessions to attract potential customers. Technology transfer demands are a form of payment, as General Electric discovered when it attempted to stay ahead of China's demands for technology for its advanced turbines. GE looked the other way when local companies imitated the intellectual property of multinational. This is another form of payment. These payments allowed the technology to spread widely to Chinese firms, where it created or stimulated competition for the multinationals, and ultimately cut into the multinational's profit margins. Of course the wide spread availability of technology to many Chinese firms may cause dramatic price falls, and consumers, including those in the West, become the primary beneficiaries. With large-scale manufacturing, local customers can also buy manufactured goods at a very low price.

Multinational companies charge very high prices from customers in India

In some sectors in India, many multinational companies charge very high prices from local customers. They are not interested in exporting their products, as they have a very lucrative local market in India. They are selling the products to the rich people for whom money is no consideration. Indian indigenous distributors are available to multinationals to sell their products at a large profit margin. In spite of huge sales in India, some companies do not want to manufacture in India.

The Chinese over saved, the North Americans, Europe (and India) over consumed. The Chinese government had discouraged spending and encouraged savings, in part as a way to ensure that inflation stayed low and their currency stayed devalued – which made Chinese goods cheap and attractive to the Western consumers.

Despite huge growth, Chinese households and corporations have been very cautious. They bank about half their earnings. Such extreme thriftiness in combination with high growth led to China's accumulation of a vast new pool of capital. It is not in the interest of countries in North America to have a very big negative balance of trade with any country of the world. It is best to spread the risk and have a presence in dissimilar markets and suppliers. It is also not in the interest of China to have such a big surplus. They will have to increase domestic consumption.

Political or natural disaster in the supplier's country can be very dangerous for the importer's economy. Although trade is very important for the world economy, balance of trade is equally important for countries. The best way is to develop import and export with many countries. Multinationals can be of great help in this development. The US should have a new and innovative look at the export market. This includes: Aviation products, light rail transit system, the latest locomotive engines by GE, signaling, communication system and electrification. This should also include traction power supply, overhead lines and equipment and numerous other technical (high technology manufacturing) items which should be exported from USA to China, India, Brazil, Russia, South Africa and other countries on a bigger scale. So that balance of trade can be achieved.

Solar and Wind energy for coastal geographically remote locations

The Indian Government should try to satisfy the energy needs of far-flung places with renewable power and energy efficiency that could be generated on site, rather than the government providing kerosene oil for cooking and lighting lamps at subsidized rates. People in one-third of Indian villages have no electricity. Solar and wind energy will be necessary for them. Moreover, there will be no lobbyists against renewable energy, like in USA and other advanced countries -- because India has a shortage of electricity and could use double the electricity it produces today.

India can skip an entire generation of technology advances and install wind turbines and solar (photovoltaic) power immediately in remote villages. Currently, 350 million people do not have electricity in rural India. India can leap frog in this essential field. The whole world should join together to produce enough electricity with renewable energy for the benefit of people around the world.

The world requires leadership, innovation, and collaboration in energy-efficiency and alternative sources of energy -- or everybody is going to lose big.

These are areas where US, Canada and Europe have an advantage.

- US should export products that save fuel with pollution free railway engines and also refurbish engines to improve their CO2 emission.

- Produce and export energy producing devices like solar panels and wind turbines, with constant improvement through research and development.

- Until a breakthrough is found in clean power, the world must dramatically improve our energy efficiency. Invent all the clean power and energy efficient tools. The clean power tools will be the next great global industry. The countries which make more of them and sell more of them will have a competitive advantage. The more energy productivity we bring about today, the fewer clean electrons we will need to generate.

- USA should develop knowledge-intensive clean power technology jobs. Unlike many other jobs, knowledge-intensive green collar technology jobs will not be outsourced and will be the technology of the future.

Growth of US export market with enterprising ways of doing business

There is a very big market in India for railways that are in urgent need for improvement. Indian railways need fast, efficient pollution free locomotives. India needs improvement in railway stations, railway tracks, signals and better safety devices. Indian railways are one of the biggest networks in the world. It is not that India does not have good engineers in railways. As a matter of fact, Indian railways have one of the best management system and engineers in the world. But with the present speed of progress they can't achieve in 30 to 50 years what can be achieved in next 5 years with business cooperation with the USA, Canada and other European countries. In the next 5 to 10 years, GE will come out with another better fuel efficiency and pollution free locomotive. The engines with today's technology should be exported and old technology engines should be upgraded or rebuilt. A pollution free environment is needed during this time, and time is of the essence. Extra ordinary efforts are needed at extra ordinary times.

India needs the best locomotives available in the world. At present there is so much pollution generated by railway engines. Indian Railways should reduce fuel consumption and pollution to half. This can be done by buying engines manufactured by General Electric, that already has a presence in India and the CEO of General Electric visits India from time to time. There is a need for a meeting between the GE president, the Prime Minister of India and the Railway Minister of India. India should buy 250 to 300 railway engines from the USA and work out some arrangement to refurbish other locomotives with them.

It is a win-win situation for both India and the USA. This is the best time for the USA and India to do more business with each other. As India and USA currently have great relations. Ideally, all the locomotives should be replaced by Indian Railways with new engines or rebuilt engines. It is not possible to replace all these with new engines in the next five years because of the financial constraint and therefore there is a need to rebuild the balance of the locomotives.

General Electric is manufacturing big GE OL' locomotive engines in Erie, Pennsylvania (USA). These huge GE industrial sized diesel engines pull long trains. These high standards helped to drive the innovation of a big train engine that spewed out less pollution, while increasing fuel economy and thereby lowering CO_2 emissions in the process. GE's engines are larger, more robust handling higher firing pressure in the cylinders, with new materials, new designs, and new pistons. It has better reliability, lower emissions, and more miles per gallons of diesel –all at the same time.

GE Transportation is exporting locomotives to railroad companies worldwide, including locomotives to China, Mexico, Brazil, Australia, and Kazakhstan. One would wonder why a country such as China which makes its own much cheaper locomotives, thousands of them in fact, would buy from GE. The reason is that GE's railways are the most energy efficient in the world, with the lowest emissions of CO_2. GE's new twelve-cylinder engine produces the same horsepower as its sixteen-cylinder predecessor.

In addition to importing these engines, India needs to refurbish its existing locomotives and also manufacture them with the latest technology. The combined efforts will have great synergy. Moreover, to expedite the process, a lot of refurbishing work can be done in the private sector and by small-scale industries. India needs a central authority which could decide and coordinate quickly, when to induct the energy efficient locomotives and keep on importing new and efficient technology for railways. If we are really serious about the greenhouse gases and CO_2, we should look for replacement all the locomotive engines and not just 250 or 300, which India might buy from the USA. India can also buy hybrid locomotive engines from the RailPower of Canada.

The RailPower of Canada has created a hybrid locomotive that could provide plenty of oomph (energy) to move railway wagons and passenger coaches around without wasting fuel. It is like hybrid engines in cars – vehicles like Toyota Prius that run on a combination of gas (patrol) and re-chargeable batteries. The whole world should cooperate and sell these technologies to each other.

India has great scope for deploying more high powered electric locomotives. In addition to the electricity produced by the usual methods, India can produce solar and wind energy on vast stretches of land owned by Indian railways. Indian railways can also buy solar and wind energy produced by rural people. Lots of Indians would benefit when they sell at least half their electricity produced by solar and wind energy generated installations, to the national grid (for electric locomotives). This could be a source of income for millions of people. Our public sector units have the base for manufacturing wind and solar energy equipment, which can be used by railways and others. Unlike the Amtrack in USA and Canadian Pacific railways that traverse huge tracts of wide open unpopulated spaces travelled nonstop, Indian railway network has many railway stations (stops). This can be used as an advantage and Indian railways can move up from diesel locomotives to electric traction even for long distance transit.

North America's blue collar jobs and green industries

It is now a core national security and economic interest in the US to have a green America. Building an important alternative to fossil-fuel and crude oil is now a must for US. Energy experts in America are saying what the US needs is building more knowledge-intensive green-collar technology jobs – for making green buildings, vehicles, and power source – which are more difficult to outsource. This will have to be the industry of the future, as fossil-fuel energy supplies becomes less and less available. As the world consumption and population grows. Green

America, where the US government imposes steadily higher efficiency standards, forces a constant flow of new thinking around materials, power systems, and energy software. This makes the USA the most energy-producing country in the world.

North America's export to India

In the following fields export from USA and Canada can be increased considerably.

- Navigational, measuring, medical and control instruments manufacturing
- Aerospace products and parts manufacturing
- Commercial and Service industries machinery manufacturing
- Computer and peripheral equipment manufacturing
- Chemical products manufacturing
- Industrial machinery manufacturing
- General purpose machinery manufacturing
- Engine, turbine and power transmission equipment
- Semiconductor and other electronics components manufacturing
- Pharmaceutical and medicine manufacturing

- Telephone apparatus manufacturing

American's power and advantages - with high technology manufacturing

Americans are skilled inventors. Americans have won more Nobel prizes than the rest of the world combined. They invented the phonograph, color television, audio and video tape recording, the telephone, integrated circuits, and thousands of other products. They are known for their creativity in developing product ideas and for inventing some of the best technologies in the world. American companies could double their bottom-line profits and improve their success rates by making modest improvements in manufacturing new products.

Americans have more choices and advantages now. They can manufacture new products and can do most of the improvement work in the USA, or if needed, send it to their branches in other parts of the world. These multinational companies will exist all over the world. They can manufacture new products or make incremental enhancements to existing products. This can be done at one of the manufacturing units, say in India, at a very low cost compared to America. Once successful, they can use the same improvements in America, and their other plants throughout the world. With proper communication between the different departments of manufacturing, sales and R&D, this will lead to low cost and shorter cycle of products improvement.

Most of the R&D in the United States laboratories are separate from the rest of the organization. This specialization of R&D has led to extraordinary American inventions. In the past, this specialization of R&D led to America's inability to manufacture and market what it invented (because of very expensive development costs).

Research done in America's universities can produce electricity in rural India

The whole world should join together to produce enough electricity using renewable energy for the benefit of countries of the world. American universities, which have done so much research, can produce electricity in rural areas of India. Research should be used for their own purposes, or for places where there is a lot of demand. If they don't, their research will go to waste, as other countries will catch up. As they (American companies) progress in manufacturing solar panels and wind turbines, they can also update their own industry in the USA when the government policies become more favorable, without the opposition from lobbyists. The world requires leadership, innovation, and collaboration in energy-efficiency and an alternative source of energy, or everybody is going to lose big. The world requires a whole new approach.

Until a breakthrough is found in clean power, the world must dramatically improve its energy efficiency. The world must invent all the clean power and energy efficient tools possible. The clean power tools will be the next great global industry, and the countries which make more and sell more of them will have a competitive advantage. The more energy productivity we bring about today, the fewer clean electrons we will need to generate. The USA has the best universities and best research institutions. If not exported, today's products will become obsolete, as with research new products will come in to the market.

With competition, every American company will be forced to develop a much better understanding of its' strengths and will invest its resources in developing and sustaining superiority in that area of unique knowledge, skill, or capability. Americans will have to drive labor costs out of the productivity equation by developing highly skilled employees and design jobs and work processes in such a way that American workers can leverage their skills to create high-value products and services that justify the wage differential. There is a need for consistent and constant innovation by multinationals in the USA. Their branches can still keep producing products with cheap labor costs in other countries. These innovative products will command premium prices in the global marketplace. To have the whole scenario work, worker skills have to be drastically upgraded and further revolutionize the workplace in dramatic ways.

American multinationals have a competitive advantage in India. America has so many business management workers, many of whom are from an Indian background, and educated and trained in the USA. They know the business culture of the USA and language, culture and market of India. The business language of India is English.

The economic dysfunction in America today is not the reflection of cultural decay. It is the consequences of specific government policies (similar to Indian democracy and government policies). The advantage of America is that they are a developed, rich country and has been developing consistently for the last 200 years.

Democracies should come together

Take a look at the attitudes of Indians towards foreign companies. A large number of Indians feel that these multinational companies have a positive impact on India. India has been suspicious of Western multinationals. This suspicion and unease has some basis. It was colonized by the English corporation, the British East India Company. The world has globalized and changed. India now has positive views of multinational companies. Therefore, the change America wanted for a very long time is happening now. America should see how they could benefit from this change.

India is going down a very well-travelled and known path to development and prosperity. It should not shy away from taking advantage of this opportunity. Labor-intensive low to medium manufacturing technologies with bulk deployment of capital is an obvious area that India can benefit from. India will now copy China and begin building massive factories employing tens of thousands of workers. India will sustain very high GDP growth rates by re-enacting the East Asian miracle. It is to be expected that India's role in the world will grow over the next few decades. With a young population, India has an advantage. This demographic dividend is time-bound for all countries including China and India. The integration of India into the world is going to be just as exciting as that of China and all its predecessors. America can benefit from this change also.

India has not used its abundant, cheap labor to speed up its labor-intensive manufacturing activities. Unlike China, which started out by selling cheap toys, clothing and apparel (t-shirts), India's manufactured export includes complex automobile parts, and pharmaceuticals. India has large numbers of cheap labor and therefore should normally be expected to specialize in activities that use bulk labor. It is no wonder that India's labor is still in abundance and still very cheap.

This chapter highlights the importance of multinational companies to improve the efficiency of the USA and export to other parts of the world. This book then looks at how to use the advantages of America's field of research to their advantage, before their latest research becomes absolute. The book also explores the export of American products to markets like India, Brazil, South Africa, Russia and China.

The First part diagnoses and suggests how India can meet the challenge of unemployment, education, vocational training and infrastructure. The rest of the book entails how to make it happen. This book is not meant to undermine India's progress in the last twenty years. This book is written to encourage and suggest how to increase the speed and volume of progress, especially for the majority of people in rural areas. India is known for its 'Jugad' (economical innovative ways). Transforming rural India is a challenge that should be focused on by the best Indian minds. It's the single largest barrier in making India a developed country. Economists proclaim that if the investment in education were doubled, the growth rate of GDP would increase considerably. By providing education and vocational training to the rural regions of the country and encouraging labor intensive industries in these locations, India can become a developed country sooner than imagined.

Summary

Today, India is one of the most exciting emerging markets in the world. India's dynamic and highly competitive service sector has long been the backbone of its economy.

India has improved its foreign exchange position considerably. India's foreign investment policy has been formulated with a view to inviting and encouraging investment into India. The West (Europe and America) and East Asians are now interested in establishing factories in India. The Government of India welcomes the investment (FDI) from these countries. There is large scope for manufacturing industries especially in India. In next 5 to 10 years India will have very high domestic savings that can be reinvested. In India, there are millions of people who aspire to lift themselves out of poverty. India is in a process of uplifting the rural masses and providing jobs to them.

India is a land of opportunity for a foreign investor. India has an open door policy now. Multinationals should have greater choices. India should also encourage and rely on Indian expatriates to provide capital. India should also invite successful, emotionally connected groups of individuals who are willing to give back to India. In India, the central government should give the states incentives to help attract foreign investors.

India provides an attractive package to potential investors. India's democracy, stability, Rule of Law and courts system assures investors that their money is safe.

The FDI euphoria is far greater in China than in India. In some sectors in India, many multinational companies charge very high prices from the local customers. In spite of huge sales in India, some companies do not want to manufacture in India.

Currently, 350 million people do not have electricity in rural India. India can leap frog in this essential field with foreign investment. There is a very big market in India for Indian railways, and an urgent need for improvement. India needs the best high powered long haul locomotive engines in the world from GE. General Electric already has a presence in India and the CEO of General Electric visits India from time to time. There is need for a meeting between the General Electric CEO (and CEOs of other multinationals), the Prime Minister of India and the Railway Minister of India. Many innovative ways of improving the railways can be explored, discussed and found.

American universities, which have done so much research, can produce electricity in rural areas of India. American multinationals have a competitive advantage in India. India now has positive views about these multinational companies. India will sustain very high GDP growth rates by re-enacting the East Asian miracle. With a young population, India has an advantage. This demographic dividend is time-bound for all countries including China and India. India is known for its 'Jugad' (economical innovative ways). Transforming rural India is a challenge that should be focused on by the best Indian minds. It's the single largest barrier in making India a developed country. By providing education and vocational training in the rural regions of the country and encouraging labor intensive industries in these regions, India can become a developed country sooner than imagined.

Conclusion

Conclusion

Conclusion -- Action needed in 12th Five Year Plan

India's top priority should be to create millions of jobs for its young, unskilled and semi-skilled population. That will be possible only if it makes huge strides in manufacturing. For this to happen, India will need to spend huge amounts of money in rural areas. We need a complete overhaul of 12th Five Year Plan.

Instead of some patch work – and giving a little bit of money here and there, to rural areas, we ought to give half of India's budget allocations to rural regions. This accelerated economic progress period should be from 2012 to 2020. No time can be lost. We have to consider 2012 – 2013 as the beginning of a new era of financial independence for all Indians, especially people living in the rural areas. Special meetings of National Development Council (NDC) and Planning Commission need to be held.

A better world starts with hopes, planning and imagination. We should think big, as big as we dare to imagine. Let us dream of the wildest possible possibilities – and then pursue them. As more of us agree on what we want to achieve, the quicker we can reach our goals of economic freedom. Once we know where we want to go, getting there will be much easier and faster. At least two major political parties in India have a responsibility to see that all Indians get economic freedom. They should forget their petty differences and share the power and responsibility together to see that their countrymen get economic freedom in next 10 to 15 years.

There are areas where direct investment is needed by the Central Government to create jobs in manufacturing industries and construction projects in rural India during the 12th Five Year Plan.

Government ought to invest directly in rural areas

(1) Seed money from the Central Government is needed for creating New Towns in the hubs of potential rural growth areas. To create work spaces, set up industries, increase jobs and provide for new homesteads and apartments at affordable costs, within reach from existing rural settlements, decongest slums in big cities.

(2) Some money must be allocated to Public sector units to multiply production.

(3) Conserve water (by drip irrigation, as in Persian Gulf countries), watershed and rain water management, plantation of trees (reforestation) to improve the environment, and promotion of essential precision agricultural tools for modern farming.

(4) Vocational training for the young to attain familiarity with using tools, so that they can readily adapt to training for skilled jobs.

(5) Education must go beyond 'reading – writing – arithmetic', to prepare youth from villages and

semi-rural *kasbahs* to constitute the work force to build new towns.

(6) Providing electricity by solar and wind energy utilization and improving the environment

Government does not have to invest (but use its authority to guide and direct)

(1) Invite and encourage Banks to extend Microcredit in rural areas

(2) Encourage private and public sector units to set up in rural areas

(3) Invite and facilitate multinational companies to start-up

(4) Attract the interest of the widely scattered Indian expatriate Diaspora.

Half of the Government's budget should go to 75% of the poor

The key to jobs is investment. India needs massive amounts of capital investment in core areas. About 100 new towns are needed to be planned for during the 12th Five Year Plan years.

Infrastructure for at least 20 new towns ought to be aimed at, for each year. Since urban areas are centers of industrial and business activities – in the light of economies of scale, more new towns should be established as hubs – or seeded amidst village groupings.

They will provide non-farming job opportunities for youths of its rural hinterland, while stemming migration to the large cities.

The need of the hour is to freeze the salaries of the Central and State Government employees for 5 years. This is because people in rural areas are making a mere fraction of the money that organized sector employees earn. There should be all round austerity measures in big cities and organized sector employment establishments. Salaries, pensions and dearness allowance of government employees have increased many-fold in the last 25 years for current and retired employees.

India has not used its abundant, cheap manpower to speed up its labour-intensive manufacturing activities. The country ought to manufacture and sell less expensive toys, clothing and apparel – T-shirts and tops – for the huge home market and for export. India would normally be expected to specialize in activities that use bulk labour.

Rationing of jobs is needed in rural areas, in addition to wider implementation of the National Rural Employment Guarantee Act (NREGA). As more jobs become available in rural regions, the need for NREGA and rationing employment will decrease. This NREGA allocation then could be redirected to education, for salaries to widely needed teachers' assistants.

While rationing of rural industrial jobs is proposed, these jobs and their duration ought to be 150 to 200 days a year. As they would be on higher pay than the

Conclusion

Indian Government sponsored NREGA. This will lead to permanent skilled jobs in the future.

Rationing of industrial jobs – to enable a larger number of young people to acquire skills – in the initial stages of India's rural development will bring distribution of prosperity to hundreds of millions of people. Pressures from the local authorities to maximize employment are missing in India, as is for Industrialization in rural areas.

(1) New Towns in rural regions

India needs to build hundreds of new towns – and base the economy of these towns on a combination of fields including agriculture, introduction of new farm practices, manufacturing, construction of homesteads, apartments and provision for services. The basic model is simple.
Let us say a developer acquires a sufficiently large piece of non-prime, inexpensive non arable land for a new town to be created close to a cluster of villages. The seed money for the new town will come from the Central Government.

The developer could be a public – private consortium, that makes forward looking improvements. Such as laying out infrastructure and adding utilities, public facilities, drainage, access roads and buildings. Then it proceeds to get a few big commercial interests and anchor tenants to locate themselves on the development underway – and sell or rent out sub-divisions to whoever wants it. Hundreds of new builders and construction firms will come into these regions. The new towns ought to be built first, in economically backward States.

Improvements to the land would begin – and as the work proceeds stage by stage, small bits are sold off to interested parties to pay for the on-going developmental activities. Office spaces, apartment buildings and factories could be built on this land. The anchor firms will expand their facilities and output. This is in the light of anticipation that the economy will grow rapidly – as the new towns are being built.

All kinds of service providers will move in to these areas, from schools, colleges, hospitals, vocational training institutes, to shops, Banks and bakeries. With sufficient income for the workers, who will buy the agricultural and manufactured products, housing and service units. There will be all round growth. Employed workers will use their income to buy food and rent housing, which will become affordable. Apartments will be available and many people from big city slums will move out there, provided job opportunities are perceived.

Farmers want the Government to encourage setting up of factories in towns near their villages, in order to enable their children to earn a decent and regular income. Most villagers want to earn non-agricultural incomes. They want to find jobs in other sectors in new towns, where they can be assured of at least some money at the end of the day or month.

Indian Railways have extensive lands everywhere. Railways ought to build 3 star transit hotels in new towns. The State Governments could build inspection quarters; also Public Sector units ought to build inspection night stay facilities in the new towns or rent houses. They should not build palatial buildings or

Conclusion

inspection bungalows in new towns. If needed, the Government could build and rent out 3 star hotels and not 5 star hotels in these new towns. Railways could also locate its maintenance activities near new towns. New airports should be envisaged to serve new towns, that have the perceived potential of growing into cities.

(2) Public and Private Sectors are integral parts of the Indian economy.

India needs expansion of public sector industries in addition to private sector ventures to provide jobs, especially in outlying rural regions. The Indian industrial sector is very small, compared to the Chinese industrial spread.

India's public sector is very healthy now. Public sector units could multiply in rural areas. Government should encourage Public Undertakings to double and quadruple their manufacturing activities in rural India. Complete austerity should be observed in these units.

Previously most employees in these public sector undertakings benefited from favorable terms of employment in companies. Now the same benefits can be spread over to the people of new towns in the hubs of village clusters. This will create jobs in small towns and lift the economy of the region. Awards should be given to the units which expand and diversify the most, in backward districts.

Encouragement ought to be accorded to promote collaboration with multinational companies. For with foreign collaboration, Public Sector companies would improve production of their manufactured goods. There are many promising locations where goods like computer hardware, Solar energy panels, wind energy turbines and other labour intensive products can be manufactured in Public Sector units.

Indian Public Sector industries can generate a lot of profit and promote rural employment. This can be effectively done by putting a cap on the salaries of top and middle level employees and limiting their numbers. In these industries, labour could be tripled by manufacturing more products. Manufacturing should be diversified in different sectors. On experimental basis, rural labour ought to be temporary – while, restriction of work days would allow a larger number of persons to learn and benefit from assured paid employment.

(3) Indian agriculture will coexist in villages with manufacturing and services.

Nine hundred million people in villages cannot survive on agriculture alone. In clusters of villages or in mini new satellite towns, the industries and service sectors will play a major part in lifting the local economy.

India needs to develop holistic plans of action for management of water shortage and rainfall instability. Efficiency of water use in agriculture is needed with new irrigation strategies. Increased productivity in agriculture, water wastage prevention and obtaining more *'crop - per - drops,* is necessary.

Conclusion

Due to lack of adequate funds, small farmers are still using traditional methods of irrigation and farming. Microcredit ought to be provided by the rural Banks for this purpose. The use of superior technology, such as drip irrigation, water collection, assured timely farm to market transportation and precision application of fertilizers are required, to obtain better output and higher profits. Special incentives should be provided for dry-land cultivation including the development and wider availability of drought-resistant seed varieties.

Reforestation is the best method known to mankind to stop climate change. Hundreds of millions of trees ought to be planted throughout rural India. Wherever possible, fruit trees suitable for a particular region, should be extensively planted. The National Rural Employment Guarantee Act (NREGA) should pay for these jobs.

In India a very large percentage of the harvest rots in the fields or standing crops are damaged before reaching the marketplace. Massive Foreign Direct Investment (FDI) and private sector investment is needed to meet infrastructure augmentation needs in India, to improve the farm-to-market supply chain. Private sector must play a big role in creating infrastructure, warehouses for sheltered storage, cooling and packaging, refrigerated vans, fleets of trucks.

(4) Employment with vocational training

In India, vocational training programs will help millions of unemployed and underemployed adults attain better job prospects and wages. Vocational Education

India At The Crossroads

System – learning to work with tools – will increase job prospects. Multinational companies will pour billions of Dollars into the widely known to be stable Indian economy, provided they are welcomed into India (the same way as China does). They will take advantage of the country's affordable labour and the huge domestic market potential. These companies will recruit local manpower and impart intensive training.

India should introduce more vocational training centers and institutes for the large masses of youth coming out of schools. It would be appropriate if students are taught to use their hands and learn useful skills, as a part of the middle and high school syllabus. This can be taught as an extra-curricular activity, which students are always interested in and enjoy, while being groomed for higher technical skill requirements in future.

Vocational training with apprenticeships and internships in companies and industries, are very popular in Germany and 14 former Soviet Union countries – diligently adhering to the salutary Russian practical training system. That requires every school leaving teenage boy to get used to getting his hands dirty – and to have his own handyman tool box.

This way, the manufacturing industry, business and trades, receive low cost manpower for two to four years, while the youth acquire required skills for a new trade – both from on-the-job as well as learning theory in the Vocational Training Institutes. This combination produces keen to learn youths with potential to move on and acquire world-class technical skills.

(5) Education

Rural India needs a lot more teachers and teachers' assistants. The number of teachers must be increased considerably for students to receive an acceptable quality of education with adequate one-to-one interaction. A very large number of teachers' assistants ought to be deployed. These teachers' helpers could be paid by the National Rural Employment Guarantee Act (NREGA).

The ground reality in India is that, most Government and Municipal teachers for rural schools and *kasbahs* – semi rural market towns – are recruited in towns and cities. They seldom move residence to their work place environs or want their own children to go to the rural schools. They commute daily to the place where they are assigned to teach.

Town to village bus services do not operate on scheduled times. The regular teachers often reach late or do not turn up to take classes. Children like to be recognized as individuals – and crave personal attention of their teachers. Slow learners particularly need person-to-person communication. There is therefore imperative need to appoint teachers' assistants.

They ought to be recruited as temporary or assistant teachers from the local resident community or living within reasonable distance from the schools. So that the children coming to school are taken care of and helped through the day's lessons. The same arrangement is needed to expand the crucial night schools system, where eager learners lose heart and drop out, due to irregularity of commuting teaching personnel.

Temporary teachers do not have to be fully trained. Even grade 10 or 12 students can get 'on the job training' as a teachers' assistants. Ultimately more teachers will be trained. In the absence of regular teachers prerecorded tapes, CDs, DVDs can be shown to students in almost all subjects. In addition to class room studies, to reinforce learning for these subjects, for the benefit of the weaker students. Teachers' assistants can play these tapes, CDs and DVDs to students in the class rooms or school library.

A well-structured vocational education system will increase job prospects. General vocational training classes should be started in schools as a part of the curriculum. Once a week, classes ought to be devoted to vocational training – getting students to learn working with tools and used to getting their hands grimy.

The time must come when like in North America, Western Europe –and 14 satellite countries in Eastern Europe and Central Asia, which gained freedom from Russia with the chaotic events from 5 September to 21 December 1991, leading to the collapse of Communism and the Soviet Union – every young man in India would strive to own a kit of basic hand tools.

Indian vocational training initiatives to draw in drop out students, should aim at ensuring their continuing

Conclusion

attendance with attention retaining short duration courses of three to six months, to get them started on technical trades. Let us build this system from the ground up on a very extensive country wide scale.

After the massive inflow of refugees consequent on partition of the Indian sub-continent in 1947 to carve out Pakistan, Industrial Training Institutes (ITIs) were set up in all rehabilitation colonies in northern India, to train those whose schooling had been disrupted, to use their hands. The result was quick job placements. For decades later, men of that generation were seen walking in and out of hardware stores and timber stack yards, while others were forever calling in repair men to fix equipment malfunction problems in their homes and offices.

(6) Solar and wind energy equipment

The costs will continue to decline as the production volume of solar power panels and wind energy turbines increase. Given India's and China's enormous populations, the number of solar panels and wind turbines required would be very high and therefore bring the generation cost per watt down significantly.

Currently, solar and wind energy equipment are in short supply throughout the world. Our public sector units have the manufacturing base, the credibility to raise huge amounts of low interest financing from Banks. Besides, cheap labour is available to them in rural regions to produce solar and wind energy equipment – and energy efficient tools.

Electricity can have a dramatic impact on education and literacy. In rural India, approximately 350 million people do not have electricity. Children can study at night after they have completed their daily chores in taking out herds to graze, back yard animal husbandry, farming, collecting firewood, drawing water from wells, playing *second mother* to younger siblings, cooking and housekeeping. Facilitating night study will help increase academic success, leading to better job prospects.

If India is to have any hope of lifting the yoke of absolute poverty, it must provide villages with greater access to electricity .That will enable the nascent network of night schools to retain keen young learners and function more fruitfully. The payback in terms of direct benefits will begin from the very first year this is put into effect.

In progressive states like Punjab and Gujarat, finding funds to give bicycles to teenage boys and girl students have resulted in significant increase in regular attendance and retention, in high schools, Junior colleges and Industrial Training Institutes (ITIs) at some distance from the villages.

Government could indirectly use its authority and influence to

(1) Invite and encourage Banks for Microcredit
(2) Encourage private and public sector production units
(3) Reach out to and welcome multinational companies
(4) Invite and facilitate Indian Diaspora involvement

Conclusion

(1) Microcredit

Indian businesses continue to grow, but not everyone is benefiting from this in the rural areas. In the absence of tiny loans from Banks, poor people regularly borrow from local money landers and loan sharks – for weddings, crop sowings and medical emergencies – who cause extended indebtedness due to high interest levied from those who are desperate for a little cash.

The Government of India could give incentives and facilitate Banks to open their branches in villages and give loans to rural people, especially the poor. Nationalization of banks was done to benefit the poor. In rural India, most people are surviving with temporary self-employment in different fields. For these people micro-loans are essential.

Some borrowers may get into trouble and be unable to pay back their loans. Due to illness in their families or other unforeseen circumstances, it may be virtually impossible for them to work their way out of poverty. This problem of inescapable debt, faced by rural community members can be tackled with the aid of bank loans, subsidies and government aid.

Banks should feel it is their social responsibility to help them. The banks could make their rules very flexible – so that they can adjust to the re-scheduling requirements of the borrower. This type of bad debts could be shared by banks, State Governments, Microcredit charities, private individuals and non-governmental organizations.

(2) (i) Transfer Government and Public Sector employee volunteers to educate and train rural people

The surplus of government employees can provide great benefits to rural India. Government employees with experience of orderly work procedures, are valuable human resources. Almost a quarter of these employees could be given the option to work in rural areas, while keeping their present jobs and salaries.

Public sector employees could be helpful in giving vocational training, education and doing project administration work. In India, there are millions of unemployed because of legions of school drop-outs without access to vocational training and education. Administrative experience of government employees will be of immense help in the rural areas.

(2) (ii) Government employees and technical Public sector employees

Training educated people from rural areas between the ages of 15 and 35 years would attract thousands of companies to these regions. Training would not have to be very expensive or lengthy. Along with basic education, mechanical drawing, plumbing, tailoring for industrial production, craftsmanship – training to work with their hands – could be imparted for lathe machine operation, welding, automobile maintenance, electrical wiring , wood working, construction work, general repair handyman ship, leather products manufacturing (including shoes),

Conclusion

catering vocations like cooks and waiters, as car and truck drivers.

Many factories will start coming to these identified rural development nodal areas, because of the abundance of available labour trained in different disciplines, following the principle, *'if you built it, they will come'.*

Vocational training can be adjusted to the needs of a projected factory and these new industries will train their employees further in accordance with their specific skill requirements

Conscientious Indian business men need to take on the social responsibility of uplifting India's rural poor. They could donate funds for capital expenditure, build new factories in backward areas and train new technical manpower by arranging vocational education.

Volunteering their own time post retirement, in addition to passing on their expertise and life experiences, if not money, for these economic resurgence causes, will be the biggest service they can do for India. Economic development in India has nurtured lots of people with money. Political leaders and people in high positions can persuade those who may spare some money, to contribute generously to this cause of education and handyman training of human resources.

During the early 1970s a dedicated group of retired Canadian engineers, small business start-up advisors, orchard planters and small town planners, took turns in living in India for a few months. Under an Indo-Canadian Co-operation program, they strove to share their training, work and life experiences free in diverse fields. They initiated light industries and other projects with Indian entrepreneurs, who were able to mobilize venture capital locally.

(3) Investment by multinationals

There is need for the Indian Prime Minister and Chief Ministers of states to be in touch with the multinational companies who are investing or intending to bring Foreign Direct Investment (FDI) to India. Also, to give confidence to the multinationals, there could be a high level committee of Deputy Prime Minister (India does not have one at present) or a senior practical forward looking minister together with the leader of the Opposition.

The Prime Minister along with the ruling party president are very powerful. Many people blame democracy for delays and give credit to China for its "fait accompli" authority, for rapid progress. But, whatever and whenever the Government of India wants to do something, it forges ahead and gets it done.

Shining instances of such bold initiatives were liberalization of India's economy by Premier Narasimha Rao and his Finance Minister Dr Manmohan Singh in 1991 – and allowing Foreign

Conclusion

Direct Investment in retail, besides the ailing domestic aviation sector, by Dr Manmohan Singh as Prime Minister, in 2012.

The need of the hour is for the Prime Minister to initiate progress faster for the rural masses. All this can be done under democracy. The leader can only be the Prime Minister and cannot be central government ministers, Chief Ministers of states – or bureaucrats. They can all be extensions of his initiatives and powers – extending his reach. With the exception of some, many Chief Ministers have proved to be very successful in their states.

In the West, many multinational companies and large industries buy up smaller companies to expand or increase their product lines. This benefits both buyers and sellers. Acquisitions and mergers is not a common practice in India. Often small production units do not expand or survive for long. In India there are not many companies which can help this acquisition process. To attract industries to projected new town locations, some initial work needs to be done by small companies or by Public Sector companies – as was done in China. Again, following the well tried out principle, *'if you built it, they will come'.*

Employment will grow significantly in the industry field, as more units are converted from public to private sector industries – or collaborating multinational companies. Public Sector units could expand and should be very flexible in terms of organizational structure. In some cases the creation of public sector units will work out to a large extent as transition strategy. Also in new towns in the hubs of village clusters, the government could give grants and tied loans to small industries. Or in some cases, work as guarantor for the small scale industry to the Banks – as was done in China.

Expenses of most foreign companies are 10 times more than those of local manufacturers, in the first few years after start up. Reducing transaction cost, is what increases the profits and makes it attractive for a foreign manufacturing company to come to another country. The transaction costs in the first few years of manufacturing are sheer losses that help no one.

Creating employment should be one of their main objectives. Many government factories will make a lot of money by entering into a joint venture with foreign partners, who will bring in new technology in production. Big acquisitions by Indian businesses and acquisition of an interest in the multinational companies will increase exports and profits of public sector companies.

India's cotton textile industry can become the largest in the world. The industry is labour-intensive and can play a prominent role in the industrial boom of the country. India creates designer clothing, but other countries copy and produce them in bulk. In addition to garments and textiles, output from light industry including footwear, toys, food processing, and consumer electronics can also be increased. They

Conclusion

can become big export earners and large creators of jobs.

High technology industries and public sector units can produce high-speed computers, different type of semi-conductors and specialized electronic telecommunications equipment. Machinery and transportation equipment can be big export earners. Solar and wind power generation equipment can be manufactured by public sector units for local deployment and export.

(4) **India should view expatriates as part of the national fabric (welcome its Diaspora with open arms)**

India can gain from the patriotic sentiments of its expatriate Diaspora, for introduction of new management practices and implementation of economic incentives – to the country's economic advantage. By consistently facilitating its Diaspora, India can take its economy forward. India should view the expatriate Diaspora as part of the national fabric – a dependable resource to stimulate the country's economic development and modernization.

A very large percentage of Foreign Direct Investment can be brought in by this group. Their wealth, technical know-how, investment, patriotism and nostalgic Indian relationship bonding, will be mutually beneficial. Indian Diaspora could provide a plethora of new ideas, followed by financing on a large scale.

The technology and industrial sector could encourage foreign educated or trained Indian managers to return home to start high-tech and manufacturing ventures. In India, by and large, its expatriates can play a much bigger role. India would do well to consider new ideas put forward and initiatives suggested by non-residents eager to be useful to their motherland within their life time.

Some ideas for reducing debt and deficit

India's Public Sector is very healthy now. Austerity measures should be used in public sector units. Manufacturing in public sector units should be doubled or quadrupled. Ultimately these units will create more jobs – and more revenue will be generated as more public sector units and their employees will pay income tax.

Best way to pay debt is to increase the pie by doubling and quadrupling manufacturing – expanding and diversifying public sector products. Private sector ventures will automatically increase with it. More taxes will be generated from activities in new towns, as with creation of vast new work spaces and civic services infrastructure available, activities there will increase income.

Earlier, instead of generating public savings, profits and output, the Public Sector had become a drain on public resources. These negative savings led to fast

Conclusion

accumulation of internal public debt and lower investment, than would have been the case otherwise. Most of our public resources are dissipated in the payment of salaries, pensions or interest on debt. Instead of on higher public investment for greater public good, this had an opposite result: higher public consumption, with diminishing returns for the public!

For the next five years more, attention must be paid to people who are earning but not paying income tax

There is a very large number, who are earning but are not even registered with income tax department to pay income tax. Half of income tax officers and their staff ought to be directed towards this group. For the next 5 years income tax officers should spend less time with people already paying income tax. There ought be less Income tax audit by income tax officers or staff, for existing tax payers. For some time, these employees should be prohibited from contacting tax payers directly or through chartered accountants.

This contact is decreasing income tax revenue, because the tax payers pay less, instead of paying more into the coffers of the government. This booty is shared by income tax officers and their staff, tax payers and chartered accountants. Many tax payers are now realizing that by paying more and the genuine amount due (as they should), they increase their capital. Otherwise this money goes into the pockets of income tax employees and Chartered Accountants – while taxpayers and the Government lose money.

Public servants' rising wages, Pay Commission and Court judgments in their favour

With rising wages, periodic Pay Commissions, and judicial pronouncements in favour of government employees, the so-called 'public servants' soon became their own masters, with little accountability to the people. As government service becomes the most attractive source of secure employment, vested interests of politicians and government employees' labour unions ensured that more and more schemes and public programs were added to the existing ones.

Administrative salaries and pensions have become 10 times more in the last 25 years. Dearness allowance increased 14 times. The lower rungs of the service, which account for the vast majority of government employees, enjoy compensation which is twice as high as equivalent levels in the organized private sector. According to some estimates, these salaries and pensions are 25 times more than what individuals among half of the country's people earn. Government

Conclusion

employees number almost 4 times more than required. This alone has increased debt so high that, hardly any money is left for development.

Role and expenses of ministers and civil servants

Each minister of Government of India is virtually a king. Central Budget allocation of funds for Ministries is like those of autonomous kingdoms. Irrespective of the Government in power, the expenses once increased, cannot be reduced by successive Governments. The number of ministries and ministers involved in actual decision making has increased substantially. It has not been possible to bring about any systematic improvement, because of the immense power and influence of special interests that benefit greatly from centralized control – at the expense of the general public.

Political leaders have gained, and are still gaining, from their control over the resources of the public sector enterprises, their special powers and ability to secure subsidies, giving contracts, and excess patronage in the appointment of officials – and incur fiscal deficits. Political leaders and bureaucrats gain from opportunities for corruption at different levels of the administration, and statutorily guaranteed security of their jobs. Individual ministers can take virtually all decisions affecting public enterprises or projects under their charge, but cannot be held accountable for the outcome.

The solution is to reduce the direct role of politicians and bureaucrats in the management of public services. The delivery of services can be vastly improved if a distinction is made between the ownership of these services (by the Government) and delivery of such services (by private and local enterprises). When the management of public services is contracted out to private groups of enterprises, the distribution and quality of the services will improve and net cost to the public will be reduced.

The other solution is to increase the size of the pie. Double and triple the manufacturing output, without increasing the top and middle level employees, (following the American expression, increase the employment of *'Indians – no chiefs'*).

This can be done by freezing top and middle level employees and the salaries of employees. Top and middle tier employees ought to travel from existing (old) factories to new factories in new towns, as is the present trend in the United States – and elsewhere all over the world – as also in private sector India.

With vocational training, familiarity with use of tools, well-structured apprenticeships and internships, the Indian manufacturing industry will receive eager to learn young low cost manpower for two to four years – while the entrants to the job market are learning a new trade. Other jobs should be rationed till the

Conclusion

employment situation improves in rural areas – and Public Sector factories start making huge profits.

Is this the last chance for India?

Since the poor are far too many, the size of the manufacturing pie needs to grow faster. Some eminent Indian economists have observed *'India is notorious for blowing its chances in economics'* Most Indians and foreigners wonder whether India will one day emerge as a major power or remain forever 'arriving'.

There has been a dramatic shift in India's economic outlook. The sources of comparative advantage of nations are vastly different today than they were 65 years ago. There are very few developing countries that are as well placed as India to take advantage of the phenomenal changes that have occurred in production technologies, international trade, capital movement, development and deployment of skilled manpower.

As a result, India today has the knowledge and the skills to, produce and process a wide variety of products and services at competitive costs. India should now eliminate the worst form of poverty amongst its people in the midst of plenty.

There is an emerging consensus that, if India follows the right policies, by the year 2020 or 2025, it would be the third largest economy in the World, after United States and China. The twenty-first century should see the dream of every Indian – 600 million of whom are under 35 years of age – to see their country as a major world power, come true.

This book would have served its purpose if it contributes to that end.

Dreams can turn to Reality: Hopeful predictions for the future of India

By the end of the 13th Five-Year Plan (April 2017 to March 2022), all villagers will have the option of non-farm jobs close to rural areas, to supplement family incomes from traditional occupations. In next ten years, about 200 new towns in the hubs of village groups may be created. Hundreds of new bridges, some airports, new railway stations and sea ports, could be built.

Large city slum dwellers will be persuaded to be relocated methodically in urban new towns. With some assistance, they may rent or buy apartments in the new towns. They will have the opportunity to find work or take jobs in the new towns. Many of the relocated would possibly become entrepreneurs or salaried workers at newly set up factories in the proximity of the new towns.

Slum dwellers can move to planned modern towns – with broad well laid out avenues, civic infrastructure,

Conclusion

schools, technical training institutions, parks, green spaces and high rise buildings.

With the great opportunity to plan from scratch, many wonderful new towns like the iconic Milton Keynes 80 Kilometers north west of London will be built. Best known planning and architectural concepts, could be obtained from experts around the world, for ever keen to see their ideas take concrete shape in distant lands.

All students in the villages will complete their 12 years of schooling. Every student will get some vocational training in school – learn to use hand tools, aspire to own a handyman tool kit and be eligible for induction in technical trades, or recruitment in the country's military services.

There will be considerable increase in industrial production – both for export and internal sales. Many industries of the United States, Canada and Europe, will have a manufacturing plant in India, as they have done in China. Prices in India will be as low as China's for export and internal marketing. There will be manifold increase in the foreign direct investment by overseas companies.

India will have solar and wind generated electricity for all isolated remote villages – besides the 350 million people in semi-urban *Kasbahs*, that do not have electricity. Renewable energy will replace the use of oil and gas. Millions of jobs will be created using clean energy technology. Sun, wind and water will be the main sources of power. Renewable energy will be

India At The Crossroads

affordable. Rural poverty will be mitigated with electricity.

Using alternative sources of energy, pollution control and reduction of global warming – will help in slowing snow melt of Himalayan glaciers, vital to keep rivers in India flowing for crop irrigation.

Relieving water shortage, rain water harvesting and watershed management for run off water storage, will help improve ground water tables. Sub-surface water levels will rise significantly, in some vital agricultural regions. Farmers will be getting more *'crops per drops'* of water. The use of well laid out networks of drip irrigation – extensively implemented by international water management experts in arid Saudi Arabia, Persian Gulf and other Middle Eastern countries – will maximize harvests with more *'crops per drops'* of water.

Contemporary 'cutting edge' technology, fuel efficient engines powering long haul rail locomotives, will be in use by the Indian railways. Fast trains will become common. Old railway stations and old railway tracks will be replaced by functional modern railway stations and broad gauge railroads.

Microcredit will help entrepreneurs to start up – or help their small businesses grow. Increase the income of self-employed people.

India will then be a highly exciting and developed country in the world.

Made in the USA
San Bernardino, CA
06 January 2013